FORREST CAPIE

Professor of Economic History,
City University Business School, London

and

MICHAEL COLLINS

Head of Economic and Social History,
School of Business and Economic Studies,
University of Leeds

IEA

Published by
INSTITUTE OF ECONOMIC AFFAIRS
1992

First published in July 1992

by

THE INSTITUTE OF ECONOMIC AFFAIRS

2 Lord North Street, Westminster,
London SW1P 3LB

Hobart Paper 119

ISSN 0073-2818

ISBN 0-255 36308-7

The Institute gratefully acknowledges financial support for its publications programme and other work from a generous benefaction by the late Alec and Beryl Warren.

Printed in Great Britain by

GORON PRO-PRINT CO LTD

6 Marlborough Road, Churchill Industrial Estate, Lancing, W. Sussex

Text set in Berthold Baskerville

CONTENTS

		page
FOREWORD	Colin Robinson	7
THE AUTHORS		10
ACKNOWLEDGEMENTS		10
I. INTRODUCTION		11
II. SOME THEORETICAL CONSIDERATIONS		13
Macro-Economic Perspective		13
Investment/Output Relationship		14
Short-Termism		15
Micro-Economic Considerations		18
Conclusion		19
Box 1: The Welfare Effects of Financial Intermediation		16-17
III. THE ALLEGATIONS IN HISTORICAL PERSPECTIVE		20
The Beginnings of the British Decline		20
Market Imperfections and Supra-Market Constraints		21
Institutional Inertia		22
IV. THE WIDER WORLD		24
The Gerschenkron Hypothesis		24
German Banks' Long-Term Interest in Heavy Industry		26
V. 1870-1914		28
Was There an Investment Problem in the Pre-First World War Period?		28
How Was Investment in Industry and Commerce Financed in the Period?		29

[3]

Demand for External Finance   30
   No Market in Corporate Control Before 1914   31
Supply of External Finance   32
   Capital Market   32
Commercial Banks and the Finance of Industry   34
The Emphasis on Liquidity   35
   The Duration of Loans   36
The Great Divide?: Banks and Industry in
   19th-Century Britain   37
   Dispersed Market Power of 19th-Century
    Local Banks   38
   Growing Anti-Competitive Collusion by
    the Banks   40
   Demise of Local Banks   40
   Banking Conformity   42
Conclusion   43

VII. THE INTER-WAR YEARS   44
Faith in Markets Sapped by Chronic Depression   44
   The 'Rationalisation Movement'   45
The Role of the Bank of England   45
(i)   The Bank's Direct Action With One Large
    Industrial Customer   46
(ii) Action to Protect the Stability of the
    Banking System   47
      The Bank and the Cotton Industry   47
(iii) A General Programme of
    Industrial Rationalisation   48
The Commercial Banks: Overview   50
   Growing Trend to Financing
    Public-Sector Debt   51
   Significance of Shift to Public-Sector Assets   53
The Nature of Financial Provision for Industry   55
   The Midland Bank and
    the Royal Mail Group   55
   A Critique of the Banks' Role   56
Conclusion   58

VII. Post-1945 Period 60
    Internal Finance 60
    Changes after 1945 63
      Bank Liquidity High in Aftermath of War 64
    Institutions 65
    The Banks 66
      Advances Ratio 66
    Regulations 67
    Inquiries 69
    A National Investment Bank 71
    The Recent Past 73
    Summary 74

VIII. Conclusion 76

QUESTIONS FOR DISCUSSION 78

FURTHER READING 79

SUMMARY *Back cover*

LIST OF TABLES:

Table 1: Ratio of Investment to National Expenditure:
Great Britain Compared to the European
'Norm' at the Same Level of Real Income,
1870, 1890 and 1910 29

Table 2: Distribution of London Clearing Bank Assets
Between the Wars (Ratio to Deposits,
Per Cent), 1923/25, 1928/30 and 1936/38 52

FIGURE AND CHARTS:

Figure 1: Financial System and the Raising of Welfare 17

Chart 1: Retained Profits/ Total Capital Funds,
1963-1988 61

Chart 2: Bank Borrowing/ Total Capital Funds,
1963-1987 62

FOREWORD

Among the numerous explanations for the relative decline of the British economy since the 1870s, failure of the banking system to meet the 'needs' of industry is often cited. It is claimed, in particular, that Britain's banks—over-concerned with liquidity—have been unwilling to provide long-term finance for industry. Banks did not form long-term relationships with companies, as they did in, for example, Germany and Japan, where it is claimed banks not only provided long-term capital but advised and generally nursed the firms they were financing; at times they even appear to have helped restructure whole sections of industry. In Britain, it is argued that such close relationships did not exist. Companies obtained their external finance from sources other than banks: they found themselves in a market for corporate control in which the drive for efficiency came from the fear of take-over. The British system, it is said, encouraged 'short-termism'. More recently, there have been complaints that the banks have failed industry in the sense that they have taken a short-sighted view and have been unwilling to support smaller firms in temporary difficulties during the recent recession.

Hobart Paper No. 119 considers the extent to which accusations of failure can justifiably be made against British bankers. Professor Capie and Dr Collins take a careful historical view, starting from 1870 just before relative decline began, and extending to the present day.

In the earliest period they review (1870-1914), the authors show that British industrial and commercial companies at that time were largely independent of outside funds for investment. The implication is not necessarily that the banks were unwilling to provide finance: family-based management was common and the demand for external finance may have been lacking because owner-managers did not wish to lose control. There were, however, supply-side changes—such as the cartelisation of banking, the demise of local banking, and a growing conformity of views (for example, on the need for self-liquidating assets) as the number of banks diminished—which

[7]

may have imposed constraints on the supply of funds from banks.

Between the two World Wars, as belief in government intervention grew, the banks were criticised for inactivity in the face of industrial decline. Capie and Collins argue that, in this period, the relationships between banks and companies were not very different from the pre-World War One years except that economic problems of the time inevitably involved the banks more deeply (if reluctantly) in the business affairs of their clients. Critics claim that the banks did not do enough to encourage industrial restructuring. However, as Capie and Collins explain, had the banks taken the responsibility for large-scale 'rationalisation' they might have put at risk the interests of their shareholders and depositors. Moreover, a major benefit flowed from the relatively cautious policies of the British banks and the Bank of England: Britain avoided liquidity crises such as those which disrupted the German and US economies in the 1930s.

Moving to more recent times, Capie and Collins identify a '. . . deep-seated belief that the City has . . . directed the allocation of funds in the economy to the detriment of industry' (below, p. 60). They conclude, however, that allegations that the banks have been guilty of short-termism are less credible in the light of recent research which suggests that any problems may lie principally on the demand side: banks would be willing to lend more if there were more prospective borrowers. Furthermore, it seems there are smaller differences between Britain and Germany in banking provision for industry than had been generally supposed. Capie and Collins point out also that, in Britain during the post-war period, attempts have been made to correct some of the apparent deficiencies of pre-war times—for instance, by establishment of the ICFC. Whatever the past differences between Britain and other countries in terms of the relationships between banks and industry, the authors conclude that those differences have narrowed considerably.

Professor Capie and Dr Collins are careful to point to the problems of drawing firm conclusions from data which, particularly in the earlier periods they consider, seem inadequate to economists. Nevertheless, by reaching back into historical records, they have illuminated current controversies about bank finance for industry.

The views expressed in this Hobart Paper are, of course, those of the authors and not those of the Institute (which has no corporate view), its Trustees, its Directors or its Advisers. It is published by the IEA as a contribution to knowledge of the relationship between the banks and industry.

July 1992   COLIN ROBINSON
Editorial Director, Institute of Economic Affairs;
University of Surrey

THE AUTHORS

FORREST CAPIE is Professor of Economic History at the City University Business School, London, and currently at the London School of Economics and Political Science. He holds a PhD from the LSE, and has taught at the universities of Warwick and Leeds. He was British Academy Overseas Visiting Fellow at the National Bureau of Economic Research, New York, in 1978, and Visitor at the University of Aix-Marseille in 1979. He has written extensively on economic history in the 19th and 20th centuries. Recent books of which he is the author and/or editor include: *Depression and Protectionism* (1983); *A Monetary History of the United Kingdom, 1870-1982* (1985); *Major Inflations in History* (1991); and *Unregulated Banking: Chaos or Order?* (1991).

MICHAEL COLLINS is head of Economic and Social History at the School of Business and Economic Studies, University of Leeds. He holds a BSc (Econ.) London external degree and a PhD from the London School of Economics and Political Science. He has held a British Academy Overseas Visiting Fellowship at the National Bureau of Economic Research, New York, and is an acknowledged authority on British banking and monetary history. His recent publications include: *Money and Banking in the UK: A History* (1988); *Banks and Industrial Finance in Britain, 1800-1939* (1991); and *Central Banking in History* (1992).

ACKNOWLEDGEMENTS

We are especially grateful for the helpful comments given on earlier drafts by Leslie Pressnell, Leslie Hannah, Geoffrey Wood and Colin Mayer. We also gratefully acknowledge the support of the Economic and Social Research Council (project no. R00023 2220).

F.C.
M.C.

[10]

I. INTRODUCTION

Have the banks failed British industry, and has that failure
contributed to Britain's relative economic decline? That
significant two-part question is, of course, topical today. But, in
fact, throughout the 20th century it has seldom been far from the
newspaper headlines. Views clearly differ. At one extreme lie
those who feel that the banks have completely failed industry.
According to them, the banks have not provided long-term
finance for investment, nor the kinds of long-lasting relationships
that would allow banks to help guide firms through periods of
distress (such as experienced by many in the recession of the
early 1990s). As a consequence, British industry has been
seriously handicapped in relation to its foreign competitors.
These critics would like to see reforms to the system that would
encourage institutions to resemble and perform the functions of
the archetypal German 'universal' banks.

Opponents of this view ask how such failure, if it ever existed,
could have persisted for so long. Could profitable lending
opportunities have gone begging year in, year out, for a century
or more? Mistakes can be made, profitable opportunities lost,
but across a whole sector for over 100 years? Another possibility
is that British industry did not seek the funds. Establishing
whether the deficiency was on the supply or the demand side has
never proved easy.

This *Hobart Paper* considers the nature of the debate and the
evidence that has been advanced. It does not pretend that there
is an easy answer. The hypothesis has been around for so long
that it seems likely the debate will not be resolved easily.

In contrast with most other studies, we examine the issue over
the very long run, from the late 19th century when the first
complaints of this kind were voiced, to the present day when
they are still receiving a vigorous airing. The study therefore
covers the last 120 years, including periods of enormous
diversity and considerable underlying change—years of stag-
nation, of deep depression, of sharp fluctuations and of growth,
and of stability as well as of several wars. It also covers
periods of many kinds of exchange rate régimes and hence

[11]

periods when monetary policy had substantially different impacts. The banking sector has been transformed in the period from one where there were hundreds of small banks to one where four or five banks came to dominate, and on to one where foreign competition obtained. Yet, throughout it all, the same basic complaint has been heard—that the banks have somehow failed industry. Our survey suggests caution in drawing such a conclusion. It also points to some of the benefits as well as the costs that go with the British banking system.

II. SOME THEORETICAL CONSIDERATIONS

Macro-economic Perspective

Apprehension over the relationship between banks and industry is derived from a broader anxiety over trends in the competitiveness and long-term growth performance of the British economy as a whole. Since at least the beginning of the 20th century, some economic commentators have been critical of the rate at which British producers have lost their share of world markets and of our relatively low rates of economic growth—and such criticisms persist to the present day. Thus, recent concern over the contraction of the manufacturing sector, high rates of unemployment, poor international competitiveness and weak balance-of-payments position is frequently presented within a long-term framework of dissatisfaction with overall growth. And it is often claimed that the rate of growth of output (or income) is less than it would otherwise have been if the UK had a more effective banking system.

The rate of growth of the economy is a product of the rate of growth of capital and of labour and of the less quantifiable factors that are wrapped up in 'total factor productivity'.[1] Within this framework, new investment is important to growth both directly through the additions made to the capital stock and indirectly through the beneficial impact on total factor productivity of the inevitable technological and other improvements incorporated within new capital formation. Since it is often claimed that both the cost and availability of finance are important determinants of the rate of investment, a link can be made between the banks and economic growth.

Both the rate and nature of investment are critical to growth. Although investment is determined by a variety of factors, it has often been alleged that in Britain's case a serious adverse factor has been the deficient nature of financial provision. The claim is that the policy, practices and prejudices of Britain's financial institutions have operated against certain types of investment—

---

[1] This can be expressed in the following conventional manner: $Y/Y = K/K + L/L + TFP$, where Y = real national output, K = capital stock, L = labour force, and TFP = total factor productivity.

[13]

and perhaps also against a _higher rate_ of investment—in such a way as to damage the long-term growth and development of British industry. Such allegations usually explicitly emphasise supply-side constraints—claiming that it is deficiencies in the supply of loans, investment funds and other financial services that prevent industry from undertaking more (or better) investment.

Investment/Output Relationship

The precise relationship between investment and output is somewhat uncertain, however. The most recent demonstration of this is given by Eltis.[1] Some countries have high investment/income ratios and strong growth while others have low ratios and good growth, which is hardly surprising since there is considerable variety in the quality of investment. For example, investment in roads and buildings has a different impact from investment in machinery. As some recent researchers have expressed it:

'Unfortunately the theory of the investment function, especially in the long run, is not one of the strongest points in economic theory.'[2]

But even if high investment went unambiguously with high growth, and low investment with low growth, the question would remain over which caused which.

The belief that raising investment is beneficial also implicitly assumes that it raises total factor productivity (TFP). However, TFP embraces a wide range of factors that impinge on the efficiency of capital and labour, including education and training, research and development, organisational structure, and managerial efficiency, as well as financial intermediation. It is important at the outset to point out that financial intermediation is just one of a very large number of factors which can affect total factor productivity.

Before turning to institutional factors we show first, in Box 1, how it is that financial intermediation raises welfare even if questions remain about the size of any gain. Financial intermediation can be expected to increase welfare by facilitating the exchange between investors and savers, and by providing secure and well-priced assets.

[1] Walter Eltis, 'British Industrial Policy for the 1990s', in _The State of the Economy_, IEA Readings No. 31, London: Institute of Economic Affairs, 1990, pp. 37-56.

[2] R. C. O. Matthews, C. H. Feinstein and J. C. Odling-Smee, _British Economic Growth, 1856-1973_, Oxford: Oxford University Press, 1982.

Short-Termism

But might there be reasons why financial institutions would *not* undertake profitable intermediation? One possible answer which has recently been enjoying much popularity is that British financial institutions are short-termist in outlook[1]—that is to say, that financial institutions and markets are overly concerned with maximising their returns in the near future, with undue emphasis on the short-term profit prospects of corporate clients. In consequence, so it is claimed, this approach militates against British companies undertaking investment projects that may involve (say) a high degree of research and development expenditure requiring a long gestation period before commercial exploitation (in the electronics or aerospace industries, for instance). If true, the serious consequence for the economy would be that long-term gains to growth and competitiveness would be sacrificed for short-term profits.

The historical development of firms has usually followed the path of individual owner, or family firm, through to the large joint-stock corporation. In the small family firm, ownership and control are one and the same. But in large joint-stock companies they are separated, and so problems of 'agency' are said to arise. What this means is that there exists between the suppliers of finance and the managers an agency relationship, where a principal engages an agent to provide some service which involves delegating decision-making authority to the agent. The question that follows is: Will the firm have a lower value in these circumstances than if it were owner-managed? There is a presumption that it will, but there is a retort—that there is a market discipline that will keep the firm in line via the market for 'corporate control' (in which there is a constant threat of take-over through the stock market if firms are not performing well).[2]

In the past the majority of firms had owner-managers (and, of course, most new firms still do), but today the most important owners of the largest corporations are portfolio investors. Managers are not normally subject to very effective shareholder discipline, since non-institutional shareholders are typically

---

1 For some recent appraisal of the allegations, see Confederation of British Industry, *Investing for Britain's Future: Report of the City/Industry Task Force*, London: CBI, 1987; A. Bain, 'Short-termism: the wrong diagnosis', *Accountancy*, August 1987, pp. 38-39; and P. Marsh, *Short-Termism on Trial*, London: London Business School, 1990.

2 See B. Chiplin and M. Wright, *The Logic of Mergers*, Hobart Paper No. 107, London: Institute of Economic Affairs, 1987.

[15]

BOX 1

The Welfare Effects of Financial Intermediation

The welfare effects of financial intermediation can be demonstrated by means of one of the most basic tools of economic analysis. Using Figure 1, imagine the case of a small family firm that wishes to expand.[1] The firm wishes to transform a part of its present income into a larger future income. Initially it is dividing its present income OY into present consumption (Yo), shown in the Figure as OA, and future consumption (Yi), shown as OB. The firm is, in other words, choosing the point M on its transformation curve, at which point the tangent shows the firm's preferred rate of exchange between present and future consumption, $-(1 + r)$. If the market has a transformation rate different from $1 + r$ the firm can seek a loan and benefit from the different exchange ratios. If the market rate is $1 + i$, such that the latter is less than $1 + r$, the outcome is as shown with the firm moving along its transformation curve to point P. It will reduce consumption of its own income from OA to OC and produce OE instead of OB. The presence of a financial intermediary allows the firm to borrow CD and so consume OD with an obligation to return EF in the following period. The financial intermediary has

[1] J. Hirshleifer, 'On the theory of optimal investment decisions', *Journal of Political Economy*, Vol. 66, No. 4, 1958, pp. 329-56.

small and far removed. But the managers are under a different kind of threat, resulting from the prospect of take-over by another company (which for the individual manager may carry the threat of loss of prestige or power, or even dismissal). It is these circumstances that are said to concentrate managers' minds on the share price (short term). The question which then arises is whether undue attention to the share price detracts from other possibly longer-term considerations that may eventually reduce the value of the firm.

A principal form of the criticism is that British financial institutions (including the banks) take short-term views. As far as the banks are concerned, this is usually expressed as a concern with liquid assets to cover short-term liabilities. Moreover, financial systems that are market-oriented (that is, where stock markets dominate) as against bank-oriented (where bank lending is predominant)—for example, the USA and the UK as against Germany and Japan—allegedly have poorer corporate perform-

[16]

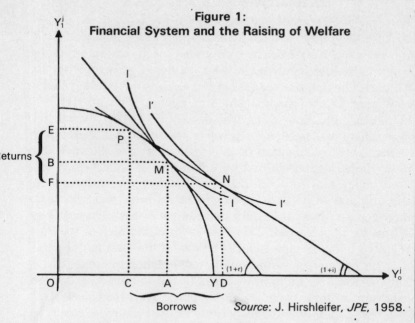

Figure 1:
Financial System and the Raising of Welfare

Source: J. Hirshleifer, *JPE*, 1958.

thus been able to place its funds at the going rate of i. The firm has re-allocated its resources according to the price structure of the economy. It has been able to move to the higher indifference curve I', that is, to reach a higher level of welfare.

ance as a result. The view is that stock market finance discourages investment and causes short-termist views and, in particular, reduced expenditure on research and development. Countries relying principally on this system have firms which are disadvantaged as compared with those in bank-oriented countries, where there is said to be a high degree of commitment by the banks towards corporate/industrial customers—as shown in their willingness to lend over long periods, to support corporate customers in periods of financial distress and, if appropriate, to engage actively in the long-term planning and investment decision-making of corporate customers. In contrast to such a system, it is alleged, British banks have eschewed long-term commitments, been overly concerned to maintain highly liquid asset structures, and have been averse to financing industrial developments.

Micro-economic Considerations

There are two types of external finance available to the firm—debt or equity. The mixture the firm chooses is called its capital structure. Does the particular composition of the capital structure chosen by a company matter? Many different structures are to be found. The question that arises is: Do some firms find it easier or cheaper to obtain some kinds of finance than others?

Unfortunately, there is no well-developed theory of financial intermediation. There are, however, some useful theoretical strands. The first function of intermediation is to alleviate the market imperfections caused by economies of scale, which are found in transactions in financial markets, in information gathering and in portfolio management. If there were no such imperfections, everyone could manage his or her own assets as well as the next person. There are, too, economies of scale in providing loans or new issues. The size of the loan may be too much for one person or institution—too much in the sense that a single person or institution would not want to hold such a large proportion of their portfolio in that asset. Thus banks can lend more easily than individuals because of their ability to invest at lower costs.

If there were no transaction costs, investors would buy their own securities rather than use financial intermediaries. Yet, even the size of transaction costs seems insufficient to account for intermediation. The small investor cannot assess the quality of entrepreneurs or find the time to monitor the performance of a firm. Ideas on monitoring derive from the existence of asymmetric information (the imbalance in information available to different parties to the transaction), which is linked to economies of scale. There could also be advantages for a bank arising from the private information it has on a firm deriving from its credit relationship. Logic would suggest that small and less well-established firms should borrow from banks, whereas large, well-known firms with a good reputation would tend to borrow from bond or stock markets.

Why might banks be the best source of medium- or long-term funds for investment? One possibility is that they represent the best means of providing the right balance in the desire for control on the part of both lender and borrower. Borrowers would like to raise finance on terms that are attractive to them, including control over future uncontracted outcomes. And lenders also need protection. The way that control can be

[18]

exercised is through short maturity, collateral, security or covenants.

This raises a central issue on the degree of 'commitment' between borrower and lender. Where it exists there is clearly the promise, or at least the possibility, of a long-term relationship. It is often claimed that bank-oriented systems have managed to harness this relationship for the good of long-term investment and growth. Market-oriented systems, such as that of the UK, are said to be deprived of the advantages emanating from such a symbiotic bank-industry relationship.[1]

Conclusion

For some years now economic theory has become more mathematical, and applied work more statistical and econometric. Apart from removing the results and studies further and further from the lay reader, the possible user, and the policymaker, even the economic specialist struggles. Some disillusionment has set in. At a conference in 1990 to commemorate the death of Adam Smith two hundred years earlier, some distinguished Nobel Laureates in economics expressed dissatisfaction with the path the subject was taking and called for a return to examination of a wider array of evidence.[2] The aridity and spurious rigour of the subject were contrasted with the wide appeal to the facts that can be found in Smith.

More specifically, in the field of finance there have been similar calls. For example, Mayer writes:

'The other factor, the closeness of relationship between investor and borrower, is even more nebulous and open to virtually no quantification. However, . . . some fascinating insights are provided by the unfashionable approach of careful observation of what institutions and people do.'[3]

This has invariably been the approach of the historian and it is ours here, informed of course by the theories and hypotheses outlined in this section.

[1] John C. Carrington and George T. Edwards, *Financing Industrial Investment*, London: Macmillan, 1979; and Carrington and Edwards, *Reversing Economic Decline*, London: Macmillan, 1981.

[2] Michael Fry (ed.), *Adam Smith's Legacy*, London: Routledge, 1992.

[3] Colin Mayer, 'Financial systems and corporate investment', *Oxford Review of Economic Policy*, Vol. 3, No. 4, 1987, p. iv.

III. THE ALLEGATIONS IN HISTORICAL PERSPECTIVE

Current allegations against the operation of money and capital markets are only the most recent manifestation of long-standing dissatisfaction with the performance of British banks with respect to domestic industry. It is true to say that banks—and, more generally, 'the City'—have often been amongst those held responsible for not doing enough to alleviate the more fundamental problems faced by the economy over the past century or so. At various times they have been blamed by financial journalists, politicians (from both Left and Right) and academics, by contemporaries and historians. Their deficiencies are alleged to have existed for at least a century. For present purposes it is useful to examine three separate periods: 1870-1914; the inter-war years; and post-1945.

The Beginnings of the British Decline

Even before the First World War the first doubts were beginning to emerge over the country's ability to maintain the economic hegemony established through early industrialisation. Long used to being the 'workshop of the world', Britain began to face increasingly stiff competition from the industrialising countries of Europe and North America. Retrospectively, many commentators have spoken of 'failure' during this period, and have sought to identify a deterioration in long-term growth trends, either in the 1870s or 1890s. This interpretation is itself a matter of some controversy,[1] but amongst those who believe that the economy performed badly, a prominent explanation has been the alleged general failure on the part of the financial sector to nurture a buoyant, competitive industrial sector.

The disruption of the inter-war years raised even more serious doubts amongst contemporaries. At that time many were in

---

[1] Sidney Pollard, *Britain's Prime and Britain's Decline. The British Economy, 1870-1914*, London: Edward Arnold, 1989, provides a broad overview of the issues; and the statistical basis of the allegations is examined in N. F. R. Crafts, S. J. Leybourne and T. C. Mills, 'The climacteric in late Victorian Britain and France: a reappraisal of the evidence', *Journal of Applied Econometrics*, Vol. 4, 1989, pp. 103-17.

favour of the banks changing their traditional business practices and more actively administering to the widely-perceived need to restructure broad tracts of British industry. For that period, too, there are strongly stated allegations of bank neglect of industrial needs.[1]

More recent academic analysis ties the performance of the banks closely to the performance of the industrial sector at various times since the War. Criticism has ranged from dissatisfaction that the banks have allowed a relatively low rate of investment to persist in the UK, to the banks' inability or unwillingness to help prevent the long-term contraction and loss of competitiveness of the manufacturing sector, and to disquiet with the attitude of bankers to struggling firms during recessions.

Seen within this historical context, current concern about short-termism is but one facet of a more general criticism that has re-emerged from time to time throughout the country's recent economic history. Dissatisfaction with the economy's general performance has, therefore, been associated with recurrent attacks on the inadequacy of the response of the financial sector to the requirements of industry.

Market Imperfections and Supra-market Constraints

These general allegations fall under two broad heads:

(i)   Imperfections within financial markets.

(ii) Supra-market constraints (constraints imposed from outside and beyond the market).

Market imperfections reduce the efficiency of the allocation process and may well result in supply-side constraints of the sort alleged to have been present in British money and capital markets. In particular, information asymmetries and imbalances in market power (oligopolistic supply) both feature as partial explanations of market failure. They are discussed in Section V.

Allegations of supra-market constraints feature even more prominently in the attack on the banks, especially within the historical debate.[2] As will become clear, although these are often

[1] Michael Collins, *Banks and Industrial Finance in Britain, 1800-1939*, London: Macmillan, 1991, Ch. 6.

[2] For instance, see Michael H. Best and Jane Humphries, 'The City and Industrial Decline', in Bernard Elbaum and William Lazonick (eds.), *The Decline of the British Economy*, Oxford: Oxford University Press, 1986, pp. 223-39.

difficult to verify, they are nonetheless fundamental to the long-term analysis of the relationship between banks and industry.

The starting point of criticism is often the widely accepted assertion that the UK has not developed the close, symbiotic relationship between banks and industry that some of the more successful economies (Germany and Japan are the most frequently cited) are said to have fostered. As we have seen, it is claimed that a close bank/industry nexus can bring important long-term benefits; it is the absence of such a development in the UK which critics claim to have been detrimental.[1]

Various explanations are offered. The broadest approach is to emphasise important socio-political and institutional constraints that govern the market practices of British banks.[2] It is claimed there are major conflicts between the objectives and interests of two of the country's leading economic élites, bankers ('the City') and industrialists. Thus it is argued that for more than a century British financial institutions have been much more involved in international finance—from the operation of the 19th-century Gold Standard, through the development of the Sterling Area from the 1930s to the 1960s, to full participation in the Euro-currency markets of the past two decades—than the banks of other advanced nations. This large external interest has, it is said, meant that British banks' businesses and profits have been less closely tied to the performance of domestic industry than those of their overseas counterparts, especially on the Continent and in Japan. More generally, it is also claimed there have been serious differences over broad economic strategy with, for instance, British financial interests showing a greater commitment to free trade, stable exchange rates and open financial markets than may have always been in the best interests of British industry.[3]

Institutional Inertia

A central element in the case against the banks is the concept of institutional, or even social, inertia—that once certain patterns of

1 Harold Lever and George Edwards, 'Banking on Britain', in David Coates and John Hillard (eds.), *The Economic Decline of Modern Britain*, Brighton: Wheatsheaf, 1986, pp. 180-86, is a useful introduction to this argument.

2 Geoffrey K. Ingham, *Capitalism Divided? The City and Industry in British Social Development*, London: Macmillan, 1984.

3 John Eatwell, *Whatever Happened to Britain?: The Economics of Decline*, London: Duckworth, 1982; S. Pollard, *The Wasting of the British Economy*, London: Croom Helm, 1982.

behaviour and institutional practice became established they have tended to become, if not fixed, then, at the least, slow to change.

A recent restatement of such an 'Institutionalist' view argues that the high degree of intransigence is not a result of the basic conservatism of the British *per se*—after all, other 'conservative' economies such as Japan have experienced dramatic transformations—but rather of the particular set of national institutional structures that have developed in Britain.[1] Nation-specific institutions have been an important determinant of the varying pace of economic change in different countries and, according to this view, in the case of the UK they have inhibited the country's transition to a modern corporate economy.

Moreover, the problem became serious as early as the last quarter of the 19th century because it was then that a new phase in economic development emerged, with a shift from relatively small-scale batch production towards more scientifically-based, mass-production techniques. It was at this point, according to the analysis, that British institutional rigidity proved to be a serious inhibitor of change, and the UK began to perform less well than other advanced nations. This analysis is applied to many sectors of the economy but it consciously encompasses the nature of financial provision. Thus, bankers are criticised for maintaining their traditional emphasis on highly liquid assets and their reluctance to support and encourage new industrial developments. The claim is not that there have been no major alterations in the relationship between British banks and industry since the 1870s, but that once a general pattern of bank/industry behaviour had been established it proved remarkably resilient from one generation to the next. Since then, it is alleged, the most important deficiency has been the absence of close support from the banks for British industrial developments. It is this institutional divide which is said to have operated against the long-term economic interests of the UK.

[1] Bernard Elbaum and William Lazonick (eds.), *The Decline of the British Economy, op. cit.*

IV. THE WIDER WORLD

The Gerschenkron Hypothesis

Alexander Gerschenkron's essays on economic backwardness are usually cited as the most explicit source of the hypothesis that in Europe, banks financed industry and played a key rôle in economic development in contrast to Britain where they did not. Gerschenkron wrote:

> 'Between the English bank essentially designed to serve as source of short-term capital and a bank designed to finance the long-run needs of the economy there was a complete gulf. The German banks, which may be taken as a paragon of the type of the Universal bank, successfully combined the basic idea of the *credit mobilier* with the short-term activities of commercial banks.'[1]

He went on to argue that in Austria and Italy, like Germany, banks established the very closest relationship with large-scale industrial enterprise. The implication was also present that the French, with the *credit mobilier*, and several other European countries followed this model.

A great deal of work followed Gerschenkron's seminal essays. However, the general propositions advanced on the rôle of banks were difficult to put in a form which would allow statistical testing. Rarely have data been available to measure the relative contributions of financial intermediaries to the financing of investment, or sufficient to show how bank assets are broken down between loans to industrial borrowers and others. Until such data are collected, analysis has to rely upon accounts derived from a variety of approaches. These turn out to be ambiguous on the validity of the Gerschenkron hypothesis.

In a study of the relationship between banks and industry in Austria and Hungary in the late 19th century, Rudolph concluded that banks played almost no part in providing extensive long-term credit for industry in Austria-Hungary.[2]

'The generally accepted view of the great Central European banks as

---

1 Alexander Gerschenkron, *Economic Backwardness in Historical Perspective*, Cambridge, Mass.: Harvard University Press, 1962, p. 13.

2 R. Rudolf, *Banking and Industrialisation in Austria-Hungary*, Cambridge, 1976, p. 184.

[24]

the entrepreneurial force which replaced government or individual activity in developing industry does not appear to be substantiated.' (p. 184)

Rudolph showed that the banks did provide short-term finance (much as in Britain) but that, in spite of having the appearance of the *credit mobilier*, their involvement in industrial investment was very limited, and

'. . . the idea of banks as entrepreneurs initiating development and leading nascent firms through the dangerous years of youth and adolescence must be largely discarded' (p. 191).

In other words, he strongly rejected the Gerschenkron proposition.

In an earlier study of Belgium, Morrison was ambivalent.[1] The general view of French experience seems to be that, while the early *credit mobiliers* were undoubtedly responsible for establishing close connections with industrial concerns and in providing long-running finance (similar to the finance provided by British banks—long-term but not necessarily explicitly so), by the last third of the century the links were being slackened.[2] Gille's view is that there is insufficient evidence for informed comment on early Italian experience. But a study by Cohen argues that Italian growth really began in the mid-1890s and was preceded and accompanied by important developments in financial institutions—notably the establishment of several industrial credit banks on the German model.[3] The links that banks made were with heavy industry, particularly electricity and chemicals. So Cohen was able to conclude that

'The Italian case closely resembles that of Germany during the early stages of industrialisation. The industrial credit banks were similar both in the conception of their rôle in the economy and in the manner in which they operated. . . . Italy's few large industrial credit banks met the capital needs of an expanding industry, with strong effects on industrial organisation.' (p. 382)

Thus the study supported the Gerschenkron proposition.

[1] R. J. Morrison, 'Financial intermediaries and economic development: the Belgian case', *Scandinavian Economic History Review*, Vol. XV, No. 1, 1967, pp. 56-70.

[2] B. Gille, 'Banking and industrialisation in Europe, 1730-1914' in C. M. Cipolla (ed.), *Fontana Economic History of Europe*, Glasgow: Collins, 1973, pp. 255-300.

[3] J. S. Cohen, 'Financing industrialisation in Italy, 1894-1914: the partial transformation of the late-comer', *Journal of Economic History*, Vol. XXVII, No. 3, 1967, pp. 363-82.

German Banks' Long-Term Interest in Heavy Industry

It was in Germany, however, that large 'universal' banks were said to have played the greatest rôle in promoting industrial development. And German experience has been the most extensively researched. Not only did German banks raise long-term capital for their clients, amongst which heavy industry figured prominently, but

> 'most importantly, the banks continued after the launch to nurse, advise and maintain an interest in their companies, aided by the technical and market know-how accumulated by the banks' staffs . . . down to forming cartels.'[1]

Yet much of the recent literature on the German experience raises questions over the actual contribution of these banks to economic growth. Some economic historians claim that the banks distorted resource allocation by virtue of their concentration on heavy industry, and that that resulted in a lower rate of German growth than would otherwise have been achieved.[2]

Although the United States is sometimes currently characterised as a 'market-oriented' economy in contrast to 'bank-oriented' ones such as Germany and Japan, this was not always the case. Whilst the banking system of the United States had a distinctly different development and has a quite different appearance from its European counterparts, a case can be made that it was banks with close industrial ties which were responsible for America's longest and strongest economic growth. American finance was very heavily concentrated before the First World War—much more than anything seen since the Second World War. It was sometimes referred to as a 'money trust'. In addition, there were close links between corporate boards and investment bankers. The view in the USA that this arrangement was a good one was very widespread at the time, though there were many critics of the concentration of power.[3] The argument in favour was that with a scarcity of informed investors, those skilled in assessing firms' potential were well employed in forming conglomerates.

[1] Sidney Pollard, *Prime and Decline, op. cit.*, p. 96.

[2] H. Neuberger and H. H. Stokes, 'German banks and German growth, 1883-1913: an empirical view', *Journal of Economic History*, Vol. XXXIV, No. 3, 1974, pp. 710-31.

[3] J. Bradford De Long, 'Did J. P. Morgan's Men Add Value? An Economist's Perspective on Financial Capitalism', in Peter Termin (ed.), *Inside the Business Enterprise*, Chicago: University of Chicago Press, 1991.

In summary, the famous Gerschenkron proposition has attracted considerable criticism. Several studies of individual countries have not found the suggested bank/industry relationship. Others have found at best a weak version of it. Also, where it is said to have held, there is still doubt as to whether economic performance was better than it would have been in the absence of the relationship.

V. 1870-1914

Was There an Investment Problem in the Pre-First World War Period?

The savings ratio in the UK in the 1870-1914 period—with the decadal average varying between 12 and 14 per cent of GNP— was not dissimilar to that of the two other leading industrial nations, Germany and the USA. The UK was, however, unique in the very high proportion of those savings invested overseas. At its peak, in the decade before the First World War, net UK foreign investment was equivalent to one-half of gross private savings.

The question thus arises as to the adequacy of domestic investment and the rôle of capital exports at this time. In particular, were the latter undertaken at the expense of the former? This is a highly controversial issue.[1] On the one hand, if it is assumed that capital markets were working well, then under normal neo-classical assumptions (of perfect competition, rationality, and so on) it can be argued that this particular distribution of British investment would have approached the optimal—that is to say, large holdings of foreign assets reflected the higher rate of return they carried, for a given risk, compared to domestic securities (or lower risk for a given rate of return). In aggregate, investors would have been maximising returns within their portfolio preferences.

However, many commentators (as will be shown) dispute the efficacy of market forces in ensuring the optimum distribution of investments, especially over the long term. Some of these critics point to the existence of impediments to the efficient operation of contemporary money and capital markets. These impediments, it is argued, created such serious imperfections that, in reality, markets were far from optimising.

Other commentators have raised even more fundamental objections, arguing that optimising activity by individual market agents does not ensure that the country's long-term interests are

---

[1] See Sidney Pollard, 'Capital exports: harmful or beneficial?', *Economic History Review*, Vol. 38, No. 4, 1985, pp. 489-514.

TABLE 1

RATIO OF INVESTMENT TO NATIONAL EXPENDITURE: GREAT BRITAIN COMPARED TO THE EUROPEAN 'NORM' AT THE SAME LEVEL OF REAL INCOME*

(per cent)

Date	Great Britain	European 'Norm'
1870	8·5	17·2
1890	7·3	18·6
1910	7·0	19·5

*The comparison is drawn between the investment ratio attained in Great Britain and the norm attained in other European countries at the dates (various) in which they achieved income levels similar to those pertaining in Britain at the base dates of 1870, 1890 and 1910. The result is an estimate of the investment ratios pertaining in different European countries at a similar phase of economic development.

Source: N. F. R. Crafts, *British Economic Growth During the Industrial Revolution*, Oxford: Oxford University Press, 1985, p. 63.

best served. These critics therefore effectively raise the possibility of a conflict between private and public interests over the long term. Thus, in this particular regard, it has been claimed that the 'loss' of such large amounts of capital overseas during the late Victorian and Edwardian periods could have had a serious debilitating impact on British growth by reducing the supply (and increasing the cost) of funds to domestic borrowers.[1] Some details of this debate are examined later (below, pp. 33-34), but the important issue to emphasise here is that the figures in Table 1 show a much lower rate of domestic investment in Britain than was the norm in Europe and, thus, provide *prima facie* evidence. They raise the possibility of a 'failure in investment'—but, of course, they do not prove it.

How was Investment in Industry and Commerce Financed in the Period?

It is estimated that industry was responsible for about 27-34 per cent of total Gross Domestic Fixed Capital Formation in the two

[1] In particular, see William P. Kennedy, *Industrial Structure, Capital Markets and the Origins of British Economic Decline*, Cambridge: Cambridge University Press, 1987; and N. F. R. Crafts, 'Victorian Britain did fail', *Economic History Review*, Vol. 32, No. 4, 1979, pp. 533-37 (but also see D. N. McCloskey, 'No it did not: a reply to Crafts', *Economic History Review*, Vol. 32, No. 4, 1979, pp. 538-41).

decades or so before the First World War.[1] What is not known with any degree of precision is the source of funds for such investment—not even in very general terms such as the relative proportions raised by firms from internal and external sources.[2] Nevertheless, some important features of industrial finance are clear. It is beyond doubt, for instance, that the overwhelming bulk of funds was generated from firms' internal sources, with the typical business having relatively little resort to outside lenders and investors.

The reasons for this relative independence of industrial investment from the money and capital markets are, of course, central to the whole assessment of whether the banks failed industry. In particular, it is important to know if the insignificance of outside finance was largely a consequence of deficiencies in the supply of funds or, alternatively, whether it was largely a result of the lack of demand for such funds from British industry. The next two sub-sections examine these demand and supply factors in turn.

Demand for External Finance

Reforms of company legislation between 1856 and 1861 greatly eased the means by which industrial and other firms could adopt a company structure. Partnership was the traditional form of ownership at that time, even in quite large concerns, but incorporation permitted the issue of shares and—formally at least—made it possible to raise capital from a wider pool of investors. Indeed, by 1900, the corporate structure had already been widely adopted by British industry.

However, this should not be taken as evidence of a widespread demand by industrialists for external sources of capital. In fact, a striking feature of British corporate structure at that time was that industrial firms were still overwhelmingly family concerns. Thus, as late as the eve of the First World War, four-fifths of all British companies were relatively small 'private companies'. The chief advantage of private company structure to the owners was that it conferred limited liability on the firm's

---

[1] C. H. Feinstein's estimates in Charles H. Feinstein and Sidney Pollard (eds.), *Studies in Capital Formation in the United Kingdom, 1750-1920*, Oxford: Oxford University Press, 1988, pp. 444-45. Here 'industry' includes manufacturing, mining and quarrying, and gas, water and electricity.

[2] An early exploration of the difficulties in making such estimates can be found in F. Lavington, *The English Capital Market*, London: Methuen, 1921, Ch. 31.

[30]

equity but did not 'dilute' ownership amongst a wide range of shareholders. In fact, the law permitted the distribution of shares to be restricted to a select group of major shareholders and, perhaps, to members of their families and close associates. Legal requirements to disclose financial and other information were minimal.

Among Britain's largest businesses, family-based management remained common, even where a public company (with wider share-holding and greater publicity) had been formed.[1] Thus, the typical industrial company was 'closely-held', with ownership and management usually vested in the same people. It is clear that the widespread adoption of the corporate structure did not in itself signal a sharp increase in the demand for external funds.

No Market in Corporate Control Before 1914

One important consequence of this typical company structure was that, before 1914, no active market in corporate control existed for the overwhelming majority of British industrial firms. Exceptionally, it is true, some important productive sectors—or important individual firms within sectors—did raise their capital through the issue of shares to the public. One indication of this is that, between 1885 and 1907, there was a ten-fold increase in the number of businesses in domestic manufacturing and distribution with quotations on the London stock market (and there were even more quoted on provincial exchanges).[2] It is also true that as a result of wider ownership of this sort from the 1880s onwards, some quoted companies in a limited number of significant sectors (such as brewing, textiles, tobacco, and cement) became involved at different times in a move to greater concentration and merger.[3] But these were the exceptions—for the great bulk of firms there was no possibility of being confronted by a hostile take-over bid.

The business of the London Stock Exchange was, in practice, narrowly based, being dominated by the securities of British and overseas governments and railway companies. Industrials

[1] L. Hannah, *The Rise of the Corporate Economy*, London: Methuen, 2nd. edn., 1983, p. 24.

[2] E. V. Morgan and W. A. Thomas, *The Stock Exchange: Its History and Functions*, London: Elek Books, 1962; W. A. Thomas, *The Provincial Stock Exchanges*, London: Frank Cass, 1973.

[3] L. Hannah, *op. cit.*, pp. 21-25; P. L. Payne, 'Emergence of the large-scale company in Great Britain, 1870-1914', *Economic History Review*, Vol. 20, No. 3, 1967, pp. 519-42.

accounted for an extremely small part. In 1873, for instance, all commercial and industrial securities represented just over 1 per cent of the total; and, despite significant growth, were still less than 10 per cent in 1913.[1]

Thus, despite the broader acceptance of the corporate structure in the half-century or so before the First World War, it was still the case that '. . . the industrial partnership and family-owned factory remained the typical unit in most branches of manufacturing'.[2] Typically, shares were not actively traded; legislation required companies to make public only a minimal amount of financial and other business information and, because of family and other personal ties, equity was generally held by people with close long-term commitments to the enterprise.

The pre-1914 system of industrial financing was therefore not a market-oriented system akin to that of recent times. Management and ownership were closely linked and, in that sense, the danger of 'short-termism' amongst shareholders did not exist for the generality of industrial concerns. In fact, it is theoretically possible to make out a case that the closeness of the link between management and ownership could have deterred industrial concerns from seeking external finance because this would have diluted control. Self-finance was finance without ties. In contrast, borrowing from outsiders—from banks, general shareholders, or whoever—would inevitably concede to these 'creditors' some influence over the business, if only of an indirect nature.

It follows from this line of reasoning that it was the relatively small scale of operations and the financial self-sufficiency of British industry that account most readily for the weakness of the link between finance and industry in the period. To the extent that familial and other personal ties discouraged British enterprises from seeking market funds, the observed insignificance of external finance is explained by a lack of demand rather than by any deficiency in the supply of financial services.

Supply of External Finance

Capital Market

The alternative case is that the insignificant position of industrial securities on the organised capital markets is evidence of supply

[1] Ranald C. Michie, *The London and New York Stock Exchanges, 1850-1914*, London: Allen & Unwin, 1987, p. 54.

[2] L. Hannah, *op. cit.*, p. 23.

constraints. Perhaps the fact that British industrialists had little resort to the stock markets was less a result of the predisposition of the industrialists than of the difficulty and cost of raising funds in that manner. Perhaps the agents, investors and institutions who were responsible for making the market in securities operated so as to discourage industrial and commercial firms from raising funds in that way. It is here that serious allegations of failure towards industry have been made against the City.

William P. Kennedy has been amongst the severest critics of the operation of capital markets in this period.[1] He sees a clear causal relation between the neglect of domestic industrial securities and the high rate of overseas investment, on the one hand, and Britain's poor growth performance, on the other. He claims that the composition of traded securities was the outcome of inefficient market forces. Indeed, he believes that the history of British investment at this time was one of missed opportunities—with savings being diverted into low-yield overseas assets, while domestic entrepreneurs were deprived of funds by which to exploit high-yield projects based on new technology.

It is not alleged that this unsatisfactory outcome was the result of investors acting irrationally—that is, refusing to exploit profitable opportunities of which they were aware. Kennedy accepts that in determining the distribution of their portfolios they would have exhibited normal rational behaviour. But he insists that their awareness of investment opportunities was severely constrained by the institutional framework of the contemporary financial markets in which they operated.[2] The important outcome was that British financial institutions developed neither an effective new issues market nor an effective secondary market in industrial securities.

In contrast, British merchant banks operated the world's most efficient new issues market for overseas securities; and the normal secondary market business of the Stock Exchange (and the portfolio policies of the leading institutions) helped secure the ready liquidity of such securities. In other words, there was concentration on non-industrial and overseas securities, to the disadvantage of domestic industry.

Others hotly contest this jaundiced view of the working of the

[1] William P. Kennedy, *op. cit.*

[2] Possible distortions arising from the operation of the tax system are not discussed, probably because of the relatively low incidence of taxation at the time.

late Victorian/Edwardian capital market.[1] They are much more sanguine about the competitiveness of contemporary financial markets, arguing that they were appropriate to the needs of the economy at that time. In particular, they believe that the absence of much formal involvement in the financing of domestic industry had little to do with supply-side constraints. Instead, they see it as resulting from the financial self-sufficiency of much of British industry which we have already discussed. Lack of involvement by financial institutions is not evidence of supply deficiency, but rather of lack of demand. The assumption is that if market opportunities had existed, profit-seeking banks would have exploited them.

In summary, divisions as to the adequacy of the response of Britain's capital market to the needs of the domestic economy before 1914 remain unresolved. There is general agreement that the formal market institutions normally handled little of the business of British industry. There is no agreement, though, over whether this was caused by serious supply deficiencies or whether it merely reflected the low level of demand for external finance from industry.

Commercial Banks and the Finance of Industry

The rôle of deposit banks in the provision of industrial finance in this period is, potentially, of great significance. Little use was made of formal capital markets by the typical industrialist—Britain's system of raising industrial capital in this period cannot be portrayed as 'market-oriented'. Theoretically, therefore, deposit banks could have been an important alternative source of funds for firms that found internally-generated revenue inadequate for their investment requirements.

All but the smallest industrial and commercial concerns would have been operating bank accounts, if only for the convenience of using normal retail banking facilities such as chequing accounts, remittance services and a safe place in which

[1] Michael Edelstein, 'Realized rates of return on UK home and overseas portfolio investment in the age of high imperialism', *Explorations in Economic History*, Vol. 13, No. 3, 1976, pp. 283-329; Michael Edelstein, *Overseas Investment in the Age of High Imperialism. The United Kingdom, 1850-1914*, London: Methuen, 1982; R. C. Michie, 'Options, concessions, syndicates and the provision of venture capital, 1880-1913', *Business History*, Vol. 23, No. 1-3, 1981, pp. 147-64; Ranald C. Michie, 'The stock exchange and the British economy, 1870-1939', in J. J. van Helten and Y. Cassis (eds.), *Capitalism in a Mature Economy. Financial Institutions, Capital Exports and British Industry, 1870-1939*, Aldershot: Edward Elgar, 1990, pp. 95-114.

to hold idle balances. Thus, if an industrial firm were seeking additional funds, it would have been a simple matter for the partners or directors to approach their banker. Moreover, as the equity in most firms was 'closely-held' by a small number of partners, incurring bank debt could have been a particularly attractive alternative to other means of raising funds (such as issuing shares) because it would avoid any serious dilution of ownership and control. It is true that once debt had been incurred, the borrower would normally have been obliged to meet interest charges and repayment schedules, irrespective of the firm's current trading conditions—whereas in the case of shares, for instance, dividend payments could be deferred in lean times. Also the negotiation of a bank loan might have required the deposit of collateral and the divulging of additional commercial information to the bank. Critically, however, control of the firm would have remained with the existing partners, whereas the issue of extra shares could have diluted the control of existing owners. It would also probably have involved greater initial expense and required much more preparation than asking the bank for a loan.

From a bank's point of view, the small scale of most industrial enterprises made it unlikely that the amounts involved in industrial loans would be too great to carry. The operation of a client's normal trading account would provide the bank with important information on which to base a decision about a loan and, of course, it could be made conditional on the provision of additional financial information and, again, the deposit of collateral.

Thus, irrespective of the main reason for the lack of involvement of the formal capital market with the financing of British industry, the theoretical potential existed for the deposit banks to make good any deficiency in supply. Empirically, therefore, a central task is to try to establish whether or not the banks did actively divert the nation's savings (accumulated in the form of deposits) into productive investment by lending in a substantial way to domestic industry.

The Emphasis on Liquidity

It is widely accepted that, by the beginning of the 20th century, British deposit banks' asset holdings were characterised by an emphasis on liquidity. Their liabilities were overwhelmingly in the form of retail deposits subject to withdrawal at little or no

[35]

notice and, despite a significant growth in scale for individual banks over the course of the 19th century, it was generally argued by the banks that a high proportion of assets should be held in a readily-encashable form to ensure commercial stability and maintain public confidence.

Charles Goodhart's analysis of the internal balance sheets of a number of London clearing banks over the years from 1891 to 1914 confirms this emphasis on liquidity.[1] He found that by the mid-1890s the banks were maintaining a very high (15 per cent) ratio of cash to deposits in their published accounts, and sought to hold a ratio of 40-45 per cent in the form of very liquid assets. These assets comprised cash, balances on call and short notice with London discount houses and stock brokers, and holdings of British government Consols. In the following decade liquidity remained high, but variations in the price of Consols led to a greater concentration on the other two items within the liquidity balance, with cash and money at call and short notice together being held at some 30 per cent of deposits. Even amongst other assets on the balance sheet, liquidity was still considered a most desirable attribute and this severely restricted the range of assets held. Thus, no industrial securities were held amongst banks' investments, although some public utilities' securities were held. In fact, 'investments' were dominated by the sort of government and other securities which could be readily resold on the stock market.

The other main category of assets, 'loans and overdrafts', which were equal to just over one-half of deposits, offered greater potential for profit (generally carrying higher interest rates). But they could not be readily marketed and were thus amongst the least liquid of assets. It is in this area that any search for financial support for industry must be concentrated. It is possible that a significant proportion of such advances was made to industry. However, the state of knowledge of pre-1914 banking is such as to provide little detail of the breakdown of bank lending, either by class of borrower ('industrialist', etc.) or by amount and duration of loan.

The Duration of Loans

The duration of loans is obviously an important consideration in any analysis of the rôle the banks may have played in financing

[1] C. A. E. Goodhart, *The Business of Banking, 1891-1914*, London: Weidenfeld & Nicolson, 1972, pp. 167-91.

[36]

investment in industry. In the present state of knowledge, it is universally accepted that the banks routinely provided industrial and other customers with short-term credits in the form of overdrafts and (of declining importance over time) bill discounts to finance such transactions as the purchase of raw materials and other stock. What is not known with any certainty is whether they also made good (all or a substantial part of) the alleged deficiency in the capital markets, by the provision of long- and medium-term loans for the purchase of capital equipment. Nevertheless, the little information that is available, mainly in the form of public pronouncements by the bankers themselves, strongly suggests that bank loans and overdrafts were not used as a substitute for capital market funds. In other words, the available evidence suggests that they did not supply industry with long-term finance to any significant extent. In this period the UK apparently had neither a market-oriented nor a bank-oriented system of industrial finance.

Thus, there appears to be a parallel between the banks and the capital market, with both providing little industrial funding. The analysis applied to the deposit banks has also been subjected to much the same sort of scrutiny as that of the capital market, attempting to explain the apparent divide between finance and industry. Some argue that industrialists rarely sought long-term bank finance; others emphasise the supply constraints that were derived from bank practice as it evolved in the UK. It is with these alleged supply problems that the rest of this section is concerned.

The Great Divide?: Banks and Industry in 19th-Century Britain

In the middle decades of the 19th century the main support the deposit banks offered industry was via their credit facilities. They were not investment banks. Their assets comprised a large proportion of quite liquid financial instruments (bills and the like) and their loans were often for short periods (at least formally). Nevertheless, long- and medium-term loans were also commonly granted. At that time, too, many of the banks were small and locally based and often had close ties with local businesses.

Such an approach by the banks is generally (though not universally) considered to have been appropriate to the financial needs of most industrialists in this earlier period of the middle of

[37]

the 19th century. Thus, allegations of 'failure' towards industry by the early years of the 20th century are consistent with either of the following propositions:

(i) During the 60 years or so before the First World War the banks' relationships with industrial customers became more estranged, with a decline over time in the degree of bank support provided.

(ii) Bank practice towards industrial finance remained more or less the same over the period but, as industry's needs for fixed capital tended to increase, a conservative, liquidity-conscious approach by the bankers became increasingly inappropriate.

The allegations against the banks usually contain both these elements, but most stress the former. Critics of bank behaviour *assume* there was an unsatisfied demand for bank funds from industry, and point to a combination of institutional and economic factors which could account for the bankers' unduly cautious approach to the supply of industrial loans.

Part of the explanation lies in the major structural changes in deposit banking during this period. The most dramatic were the increase in market concentration and in the scale of operations.

Dispersed Market Power of 19th-century Local Banks

In the middle of the 19th century market power had been widely dispersed. Thus, the banking system in England and Wales (the Scottish and Irish institutions were largely independent) had comprised hundreds of small, usually local, banks (such as the Bank of Liverpool and the Yorkshire Banking Company). By the close of the First World War, however, market power was highly concentrated in all parts of Britain, with the 'Big Five' (Midland, Lloyds, National Provincial, Barclays and Westminster) alone holding four-fifths of aggregate deposits in England and Wales. These banks had pursued both vigorous internal growth, through the opening of numerous branch offices, and dramatic external expansion, through ready participation in a merger movement (whose peak of activity came in the late 1880s/early 1890s but which continued until after the First World War).[1] In consequence, there was a sharp increase in the scale of

[1] Forrest Capie and Ghila Rodrik-Bali, 'Concentration in British Banking, 1870-1920', *Business History*, Vol. 24, No. 3, 1982, pp. 280-92.

operations of the typical bank. In 1875, for instance, English joint-stock banks, on average, had been running just 11 branches, but by 1913 this had risen 16-fold, to 156 branches. Similarly for the average British bank, public liabilities (mainly deposits) rose nine-fold, from £1·3 million to £11·6 million.[1] There had thus been a major transformation—from a system of local or regional banks, to one of large-scale national banks, with head offices in the City of London and extensive branch networks throughout the country.

An increase in the scale of operations, and even the greater concentration of market power in the hands of fewer suppliers of bank loans, would not in themselves have necessarily been damaging to industrial borrowers. Indeed, some important advantages could have accrued. In the first instance, the larger resources available to the emergent national banks should have made it easier to service demands from industry. Over time, the scale of industrial and commercial operations was increasing and, thus, if banks had remained small, locally-based concerns this could have imposed a serious constraint since they might have found their resources increasingly overstretched as industrial customers sought ever larger loans. In fact, the reverse was closer to what actually happened: the growth of scale in deposit banking, for the most part, took place ahead of that in industry. Increased size also permitted a greater spread of risk by allowing the banks to attain a larger sectoral and geographical coverage both for deposit-gathering and for the placing of loans and investments.

This increased ability to spread risks added to the general stability of the British banking system and this, too, carried gains for industry. The last serious deposit bank failures in Britain were in 1878 (when both the City of Glasgow Bank and the West of England & South Wales District Bank failed). In contrast, banks in other developed nations remained vulnerable to liquidity pressures even into the 20th century and on occasions when collapses occurred, this could have very serious consequences for industrial customers and the general economy alike. British stability was partly dependent on the Bank of England's ability to divert international currency flows into the domestic economy when necessary. But stability was also derived from

[1] Michael Collins, *Money and Banking in the UK. A History*, London: Croom Helm, 1988, pp. 40, 52. Also see Forrest Capie and Alan Webber, *A Monetary History of the United Kingdom, 1870-1982*, Vol. 1, London: Allen & Unwin, 1985, Chs. 10 and 11.

the banks' ability to spread risks and from their insistence on holding a high proportion of cash and near-cash assets. As a result, British industrial firms were spared the trauma of serious bank collapses.

A final possible advantage to industrial customers of institutional changes to the banking structure was that the economies derived from the sharp growth in scale should have reduced banks' operating costs. This could have resulted in cheaper services for customers, despite the trend towards greater concentration of market power, provided competition amongst the new oligopolists remained effective.

Growing Anti-Competitive Collusion by the Banks

However, despite these possible advantages, in other respects institutional change may have worked against a deeper involvement by the deposit banks in the affairs of domestic industry. For instance, there is evidence that by the early 20th century there was increasing collusion by the banks to suppress competition, which would have reduced gains to customers derived from any reduction in costs from the banks' larger scale of operations. The most direct attempts at collusion were the various cartel agreements to fix interest rates on deposits and loans, operating against all customers, including industry and commerce.[1]

In addition, the increasing concentration of banks in the City of London, and the growing independence of deposit banking profits from those of domestic producers, may have served to reinforce the divide between industry and finance. Senior management of the new concerns were now working in close proximity to all the major money market institutions of the City—the discount market, stock market and Bank of England—where government and international finance were the chief concerns, not the needs of a domestic industry largely based in the provinces.

Demise of Local Banks

A necessary concomitant to the emergence of Britain's new banking giants was the demise of local banking. This probably reduced the degree of personal contact between banker and businessman and may, therefore, have reduced the degree of co-

[1] Brian Griffiths, 'The development of restrictive practices in the UK monetary system', *Manchester School*, Vol. 41, 1973, pp. 3-18; S. G. Checkland, *Scottish Banking. A History, 1695-1973*, London and Glasgow: Collins, 1975, pp. 391-92, 486-87.

operation that had been feasible in earlier years. Whereas, in the middle of the 19th century, there had been a local banker whose own profit was inextricably linked to that of the local economy, businessmen seeking loans in the years before the First World War had to negotiate with the branch manager of a national concern. The suggestion by critics[1] is that such employees had less power than exercised by the formerly independent local bankers and that, in such circumstances, the provision of (riskier) loans to industry could have been given lower priority.

One reason for this reduced power was the necessity for administrative and organisational procedures more appropriate to the new large-scale banking enterprises. Each banking conglomerate was an amalgamation of what had been scores of separate constituent banks. It was imperative that these be forged into a single corporation, with standardised corporate ethos and policy. Senior management, now based in London, had to develop and implement a corporate policy that could be applied in all branches, to all parts of the country—and this necessarily restricted local initiative. *Bankers therefore had reduced flexibility*

Centralisation also facilitated the emergence of a banking 'profession'. By the last quarter of the 19th century a body of professional opinion had developed as to what constituted respectable business and acceptable practice for a bank. This attitude was noticeably conservative and cautious, extolling the virtues of liquidity. It was partly derived from experience. One feature of the period up to the end of the 1870s was the recurrence of 'liquidity pressures' when, for short periods, public confidence in the banks' ability to meet their liabilities on demand was sorely tested. Thus, the middle decades of the century had witnessed short-lived 'runs' on the banks in 1847, 1857, 1866 and 1878. Each of these crises re-inforced bankers' prejudices against holding too many assets that could not be readily turned into cash, and there is evidence that they encouraged the evolution of more liquid balance sheets.[2] Certainly by the beginning of the 20th century, standard banking texts[3] were warning against tying up assets for long

---

[1] Youssef Cassis, 'British Finances: success and controversy', in J. J. van Helten and Y. Cassis (eds.), *Capitalism in a Mature Economy*, Aldershot: Edward Elgar, 1990.

[2] Michael Collins, 'The banking crisis of 1878', *Economic History Review*, Vol. 42, No. 4, 1989, pp. 504-27.

[3] For example, J. W. Gilbart, *The History, Principles and Practice of Banking*, London: G. Bell & Sons, 1907.

[41]

periods, and arguing the desirability of self-liquidating, short-term and readily saleable assets. Long-term loans and investments in the private sector, of course, were not considered to be amongst these assets.

The new institutional structure probably facilitated the wide acceptance of such business norms. Thus by dint of size alone, acceptance by just one board of directors of one of the leading banks of, say, rules governing the liquidity of balance sheets, or the operation of industrial accounts, would ensure its implementation across a large proportion of the profession. The new corporations could rapidly disseminate acceptable norms of practice amongst their staff.

Banking Conformity

The publication of general accounts and the widespread interest in the liquidity and profitability of the large banks also served to encourage conformity across banks, with no one bank wanting to be seen as significantly out of line with its competitors. In fact, in general terms all the major deposit banks conducted very similar businesses, as they concentrated on a relatively narrow range of activities. In the same way as for others, specialisation of function became an important feature of these money market institutions. Despite accumulating vast deposit resources, they did not diversify to any significant extent by, for example, moving into industrial finance. By the time of the First World War they were active advocates of compartmentalisation of function, making their own contribution to the segmentation that had become a feature of British financial markets.

Thus, the deposit banks remained wedded to the provision of short-term finance and their services remained essentially intermediary in character. They did not emerge as 'universal banks' offering a very wide range of financial services. In particular, they did not evolve the close relationship with industry that some banks in the USA and Germany are reputed to have developed.[1] Despite the immensity of their resources, they did not display long-term 'commitment' to their industrial customers (in the sense of providing formal long-term loans) and they did not participate in the managerial decisions of such customers. They concentrated on the liquidity of their assets and

[1] William P. Kennedy, *op. cit.*, pp. 86, 118, 120-21; R. H. Tilley, 'German banking, 1850-1914: development assistance for the strong', *Journal of European Economic History*, Vol. 15, No. 1, 1986, pp. 113-51.

kept industry at arm's length. In that sense, according to their critics, they contributed to Britain's investment problem.

Conclusion

This review of the relationship between industry, the banks, and the formal capital market has highlighted three main features of pre-1914 financial markets:

1. The low level of dependence of British industrial and commercial firms on outside sources of funds for investment. Neither British deposit banks nor capital market institutions were significant suppliers of investment funds to the industrial sector.

2. That this observed fact is consistent with two contradictory explanations—either that supply constraints were denying funds to industry, or that industry's investment demands were such that there was little need for external finance from the banks and other financial institutions.

3. One important qualification is that, despite the frequent assertion of firmly held (and, as we have seen, sometimes contradictory) views, a great deal of research is still required before the detailed nature of the bank/industry relationship is established. There is general agreement about the function of London-based institutions, but exceedingly little is known either of the detailed relationship between deposit banks and their industrial clients in the provinces, or of the effectiveness of the miscellany of small-scale suppliers alleged to have operated in the period.

VI. THE INTER-WAR YEARS

Faith in Markets Sapped by Chronic Depression

Most concern over competitiveness and growth during the pre-1914 period has been raised only retrospectively. Between the wars, however, serious doubts emerged at the time. The reason was the loss of international hegemony and the accompanying economic disruption. The main long-term problem was the sharp decline in exports and the resultant disruption to labour markets. In constant price terms, total British exports in the 1920s remained below their immediate pre-First World War level and they fell still further (by some 18 per cent between 1929 and 1937).[1] This created extremely high rates of regional unemployment in such geographically concentrated industries as cotton textiles and coal which were particularly dependent on overseas markets. Moreover, for two decades unemployment in general remained at historically high rates—averaging just under 13 per cent of the total insured labour force (about 9 per cent of all employees) during the 1920s, and some 16·5 per cent (almost 13 per cent of employees) during the 1930s. The chronic, persistent nature of the problem began to sap long-established faith in the ability of the market economy to right itself.

Thus, by the late 1920s doubts were already being publicly expressed, even amongst some of the country's leading economic decision- and policy-makers.[2] Serious thought began to focus on possible modifications of, and alternatives to, the traditional unfettered market economy. Significantly, the debate began to embrace not only the conduct of policy but also the nature of practice in both capital and money markets. In the capital market there had been a continuation of the trend towards incorporation amongst industrial and commercial firms, and the contraction of the international economy obliged some institutions, such as the merchant banks, to take a somewhat greater interest in developments in the domestic

---

[1] C. H. Feinstein, *National Income, Expenditure and Output of the United Kingdom, 1855-1965*, Cambridge: Cambridge University Press, 1972, p. T22.

[2] A. Booth, 'Britain in the 1930s: a managed economy?', *Economic History Review*, Vol. 40, No. 4, 1987, pp. 499-522; Leslie Hannah, *Corporate Economy, op. cit.*, Chs. 3 and 4.

economy.[1] Nevertheless, British industry continued to rely upon other sources for the bulk of its investment funds and—as in the pre-1914 period—the banking sector therefore remained an important potential source of industrial finance in the inter-war years.

The 'Rationalisation Movement'

An important manifestation of contemporary concern was the so-called 'rationalisation movement', and to many the banks' rôle was critical. Although a somewhat vague term, 'rationalisation' was taken to mean the improvement of industrial productivity through the adoption of new production and managerial techniques, the removal of excess capacity, and the consolidation and restructuring of the industrial process through mergers and other organisational reforms. Two aspects are of direct relevance here. One was the greater willingness to countenance official intervention in economic affairs. The second was the widespread belief that improvements in financial services could greatly facilitate the process of industrial rejuvenation. Both of these factors were instrumental in explaining the extraordinary degree to which the Bank of England was to become involved in industrial financing in these years. It is with this involvement that this section first deals.

The Role of the Bank of England

Until nationalisation in 1946, the Bank of England was nominally an independently-owned bank, although by the 1920s it was already clearly perceived as the country's central bank. Its main 'public' functions were to manage the government's accounts (including the servicing of public sector debt which had increased dramatically during the War); to hold the country's gold and foreign currency reserves; to manage the international exchange rate; and to maintain the stability of the domestic banking system (for example, through the provision of lender-of-last-resort facilities). In the inter-war years, pressure for amelioration of the economy's chronic difficulties (especially after the effects of the severe world-wide recession of the late 1920s/early 1930s began to bite) was to suck the Bank into an even wider, if imprecise, quasi-executive rôle. Its involvement in

[1] L. Hannah, *ibid.*; W. A. Thomas, *The Finance of British Industry, 1918-1976*, London: Methuen, 1978, Chs. 1-5.

[45]

industrial finance provides an important illustration of this expanded activity.

For ease of analysis it is useful to treat the Bank's involvement under three main heads:

(i) Individual action on the commercial account of an industrial customer.

(ii) Action to protect the stability of the banking system.

(iii) Action to promote industrial rationalisation.

(i) The Bank's Direct Action With One Large Industrial Customer

The Bank of England first became involved in more extensive support for industry in the 1920s. One of its most important industrial customers, the Newcastle-based armaments manufacturer, Armstrong, Whitworth & Co., had run into serious problems once the War and post-war boom had ceased. In some ways the firm's problems were similar to those facing broad tracts of British industry that had to find an acceptable means of adjusting to declining markets. As the country's central bank, the Bank of England was soon to find itself called upon to offer some form of leadership and guidance to other banks carrying similarly troublesome industrial accounts. In this sense the Bank of England's response in this particular case—involving one of its own industrial customers—represents an important precursor of its response to the more general problem.

Armstrong & Co.'s capacity had been expanded sharply during the War and now exceeded foreseeable peacetime demand. There appeared to be an opportunity to put rationalisation into practice—to implement a thorough streamlining of the company in order to reduce capacity and increase efficiency.[1] Indeed the Bank, as the major creditor, was potentially in a powerful position to exercise considerable leverage on the firm to do so. It was, however, the commonly-perceived failure of the banks to play any such part in industrial developments that was bringing major criticism down on the City—normally the banks looked to their liquidity and minimised their involvement. But in this case it seems that Montagu Norman, the Governor of the Bank, was prepared to go beyond

---

[1] The Bank may also have been conscious of the strategic issues involved in the possible commercial collapse of one of the country's leading manufacturers of armaments.

traditional limits and both exert pressure and provide inducements for the firm to undertake a major restructuring of its business. In the event, this not only involved the Bank in supplying extraordinary finance for the company (with the Bank taking a controlling interest in the company's equity), but also resulted in Bank officials and their advisers actively participating in the planning and implementation of the firm's overall business strategy.[1] On the face of it, this was a clear example of close support for industry from the country's leading bank.

(ii) Action to Protect the Stability of the Banking System

In this period, the Bank of England had no formal responsibilities for the prudential conduct of banking institutions: for instance, it had no legislative powers of the type it has today, whereby it can stipulate minimum capital and liquidity requirements for other banks. Nevertheless, it did acknowledge a general responsibility for the maintenance of the stability of the banking system. The Bank was prepared on occasions, for example, to exercise an influence over the conduct of individual institutions through personal contact (sometimes known as 'moral suasion'). More particularly, it accepted a duty to act as lender of last resort, by always being prepared to advance legal tender on sound securities to established money market institutions (which, in practice, meant the discount houses which acted as buffers between the clearing banks and the central bank).

Traditionally, such a duty was seen to add to the stability of the whole system by enabling soundly-managed banks to avoid serious liquidity difficulties—they could always get cash from the Bank in the last resort. In the inter-war period, however, the country's industrial problems were serious enough to pose a more general threat to banking stability than the short-term liquidity difficulties of a particular bank, and the Bank of England found itself drawn into much more intervention than previously.

The Bank and the Cotton Industry
The Bank's involvement in the re-organisation of the Lancashire cotton industry is a prime example of such intervention. The

---

[1] See R. S. Sayers, *The Bank of England, 1891-1944*, Cambridge: Cambridge University Press, 1976, Ch. 15, pp. 546-51, for a broad coverage of the Bank's industrial involvement.

industry was heavily export-oriented and loss of overseas markets left producers with excess capacity and heavy indebtedness. Widespread bankruptcies were inevitable, but several of the clearing banks were so deeply involved that the Bank of England was fearful for the stability of the banking system. Public confidence had to be maintained at all costs. Thus, the Bank felt obliged to take action in the case of Williams, Deacons, a relatively small Manchester bank which had made extensive loans to cotton firms, to ensure a new infusion of capital by persuading the Royal Bank of Scotland to take over the firm. It is a measure of the Bank's anxiety and of its commitment to the stability of the system that it used its own money to indemnify the Royal against any losses it might incur in the transaction. It was also scrupulous in ensuring that the real reasons for the merger were not made public.

The problem was more general, however, as many of the major banks had lent large amounts to cotton firms in the immediate post-war boom when the prospects for the industry had seemed rosy. By the early 1930s the chances of repayment seemed remote and a significant proportion of bank assets had become locked into 'bad debt'. In these circumstances, the further contraction of world markets during the Great Depression threatened both industry and the banks and, thus, attracted the Bank of England's attention. A major outcome was the setting up of the Lancashire Cotton Corporation in 1931. This institution was given the task of rationalising the sector, reducing the productive capacity of the hundreds of firms in the industry. The Bank persuaded the clearing banks to agree to the general financial arrangements, contributed £920,000 itself in the form of loans to the Corporation, added its own guarantee to an issue of the Corporation's debentures, and even purchased stock outright. In all, this marked an extraordinary degree of intervention by the Bank and—seen in the context of its responsibility for maintaining the stability of the banking system—represented a remarkable extension of the lender-of-last-resort function.

(iii) A General Programme of Industrial Rationalisation

However, as the country's industrial problems were more extensive than those of Lancashire cotton, so the Bank of England extended its own areas of industrial intervention. Indeed, in sum, this intervention was so out of character with the

Bank's pre-1914 behaviour that, on the face of it, it seems to have been developing a more general policy of industrial rationalisation in this period. In other words, it seems to have taken a much longer-term view and to have promoted a greater fusion of banking and industrial interests along the lines that critics were advocating.

For instance, the Bank was the driving force behind the promotion of the Lancashire Steel Corporation as a vehicle for industrial rationalisation. It also provided essential advice and perspective in the re-organisation of two of the country's ailing industrial conglomerates, The Royal Mail Shipping and Beardmore groups. In addition, the Bankers' Industrial Development Company, which was established in 1930, was a more general effort to divert banking money into industrial rationalisation. The Company had a nominal capital of £6 million, subscribed by the clearing banks, other City institutions and the Bank of England (which put up a quarter of the capital and provided much of the early motivation). Finally, the Bank was also involved to a small extent in providing extra resources for small business in depressed regions and, more surprisingly, for encouraging the provision of hire-purchase facilities to small firms.[1]

In aggregate, these various measures by the Bank of England represented a new degree of involvement in industrial affairs by a central bank in Britain. Deeper analysis of the Bank's motives and aims, however, somewhat temper any 'positive' interpretation of its actions. In fact, there is strong evidence to suggest that the Bank was adopting a relatively short-term perspective and that an important part of its intervention was intended to stave off interference from government.[2] In his evidence to the main official inquiry of the period, the Macmillan Committee, Montagu Norman did not argue for a full-blooded shift in direction of the banks' policy towards industry. Instead, he emphasised the temporary nature of the economic crisis which he felt justified the banks adopting a somewhat different attitude towards industrial finance, but only for the interim.[3] The

[1] C. E. Heim, 'Limits to intervention: the Bank of England and industrial diversification in the depressed areas', *Economic History Review*, Vol. 37, No. 4, 1984, pp. 533-50; Sue M. Bowden and Michael Collins, 'The Bank of England, industrial regeneration and hire purchase between the wars', *Economic History Review*, Vol. 45, No. 1, 1992, pp. 120-36.

[2] Bowden and Collins, *op. cit.*; Hannah, *Corporate Economy*, *op. cit.*, pp. 49-50.

[3] [Macmillan] Committee on Finance and Industry, *Minutes of Evidence*, London: HMSO, 1931, pp. 210-13, 294.

assumption was that once the economy had returned to a more 'normal' condition, then normal financial provision would prove adequate.

The setting up of the Macmillan Committee was in itself an expression of the growing political unease over the rôle of the banks in promoting the rejuvenation of British industry. Montagu Norman was fully aware of these political pressures, of course, and internal memoranda show that at least part of the reason for the Bank's own initiatives was to forestall government action. The Governor wanted to avoid political interference in the banking system at all costs and was therefore prepared to promote some moves towards rationalisation from within the City establishment. This was not the Governor's sole motivation— we have seen, for instance, that there was also concern for bank liquidity—but it strongly suggests fairly tight limits to the degree of acceptable intervention. It is not surprising, therefore, that while critics acknowledge the unprecedented nature of the Bank's 'industrial policy', they still regard it as inadequate.[1]

The Commercial Banks: Overview

Judgement on the commercial banks' support for industry in this period is similar in method to that on the Bank of England, in that it also requires careful evaluation of conflicting evidence. The industrial depression undoubtedly induced greater involvement with industrial customers, but in the case of the commercial banks there is even greater doubt than for the Bank of England that this involved any fundamental change in attitudes or policy towards the provision of industrial finance.

Examination of the banks' aggregate position does not, on the face of it, reveal a strong positive response to the requirements of industry. Representatives of banking 'good practice' continued to emphasise the importance of maintaining a highly liquid balance sheet, of holding a high proportion of cash and near-cash assets, and of avoiding the tying up of resources in long-term loans.[2] According to this accepted wisdom, bank lending

---

1 Critics are still more caustic about the Bank's over-concern with the external account and, in particular, its commitment to the international gold standard which is seen as having been damaging to industrial interests. On this subject, see Sidney Pollard (ed.), *The Gold Standard and Employment Policies between the Wars*, London: Methuen, 1970.

2 See, for example, Barnard Ellinger, *The City. The London Financial Markets*, London: King, 1940, pp. 143-44; Walter Leaf, *Banking*, London: Williams & Norgate, 1926, p. 157; [Macmillan] Committee on Finance and Industry, *Report*, Cmd. 3897, London: HMSO, 1931, pp. 172-73.

should ideally be confined to the provision of short-term credit (over a matter of months) and should not be the means of providing capital to business clients.

Table 2 provides some breakdown of the assets held by the London clearing banks over this period. In general terms, the Table confirms the emphasis on liquidity.[1] Cash, money at call and short notice, and bills were all very short-term assets; and 'investments' were, in effect, holdings of British government securities for which there was an active secondary market in the City. Even 'advances' consisted to a large extent of short-term loans and overdrafts—the exact percentage is unknown but the bankers themselves emphasised that their main function was to provide short-term credit.

Growing Trend to Financing Public-Sector Debt

Two features of the trend in asset holdings revealed by Table 2 should be highlighted here. First, during the 1930s the banks' balance sheets became more liquid (if cash, money at call and short notice, bills and investments are grouped together as highly liquid assets). Secondly—and as a necessary concomitant— the banks' assets became increasingly diverted to financing public-sector debt. The so-called liquid assets, in fact, were overwhelmingly forms of public sector debt. 'Investments' were long-dated government securities, 'bills' were predominantly short-term Treasury bills, 'money at call and short notice' were mainly balances left with the discount houses for the purchase of such securities as Treasury bills, and even 'cash' was another form of claim on the authorities. The total holding of all these assets rose quite sharply (from 48·5 per cent of deposits in 1928/ 30 to 58·6 per cent in 1936/38), essentially because of the rise in investments. Thus, in general terms, trend movements in the clearers' balance sheets were in the opposite direction from that advocated by those critics who called for a greater commitment to the private sector, including the industrial sector.

On the basis of the traditional classifications given in Table 2, it was only through 'advances' that the banks could be providing finance for industry. The Macmillan Committee persuaded the banks to reveal some hitherto unavailable detail on the distribution of these advances between the personal and corporate sectors and amongst different types of industries. This showed

[1] See Michael Collins, *Money and Banking in the UK*, London: Croom Helm, 1988, Ch. 8, for a more detailed analysis of bank assets and liabilities in the period.

TABLE 2

DISTRIBUTION OF LONDON CLEARING BANK ASSETS BETWEEN THE WARS

(ratio to deposits, per cent)*

Date (end of year)	Cash & Money at Call & S/N 1	Bills 2	Investments 3	Liquid Assets (sum of 1, 2 & 3) 4	Advances 5	Total Value of Advances 6
1923/25	19·1	15·0	18·7	52·8	48·4	£822m.
1928/30	19·4	14·7	14·4	48·5	52·0	£959m.
1936/38	18·0	12·9	27·7	58·6	41·2	£914m.

*Three-year averages—District Bank excluded.

Source: Forrest Capie and Michael Collins, *The Interwar British Economy: A Statistical Abstract*, Manchester: Manchester University Press, 1983, pp. 92-99.

that, on average, about one-half of all advances were granted to trade and industry, but gave no information as to the duration of such loans.[1] More generally, bankers at the time claimed they were aiming to place between 50 and 60 per cent (varying from bank to bank) of their deposits in the form of advances (both industrial and non-industrial). However, as Table 2 reveals, it was only towards the close of the 1920s that the clearing banks as a group managed to reach even the lower end of this target. More significantly, the proportion fell sharply during the 1930s—from 52 per cent of deposits in 1928/30 to just 41·2 per cent in 1936/38. Advances also fell in absolute money terms, from £959 million to £914 million.

This is particularly remarkable because domestic expansion resulted in the economy as a whole growing quite strongly during the 1930s, despite continuing problems in export sectors. What the figures make clear, however, is that (in aggregate terms) this growth was not being financed by an expansion in bank lending. Here was the obverse consequence of the greater commitment to the public sector.[2]

Significance of Shift to Public Sector Assets

Part of the explanation for the shift from private-sector to public-sector assets lies in the effects of the authorities' debt management policy.[3] The First World War had witnessed a very sharp increase in public debt of all sorts, and the clearers had been large purchasers. Peacetime checked the authorities' demands for new debt and, gradually, the banks managed to divert more of their resources towards the private sector during the course of the 1920s. However, during the 1930s the authorities were able to exploit the prevailing low market rate of interest and to conduct a successful funding programme. They significantly shifted the composition of the national debt away from short-term securities to longer debt. For example, the proportion consisting of 25 or more years' maturity increased from about 32 per cent to 40 per cent between 1930/31 and 1938/39. To the

[1] T. Balogh, *Studies in Financial Organization*, Cambridge: Cambridge University Press, 1947, p. 83.

[2] H. G. Johnson, 'Some implications of secular changes in bank assets and liabilities in Great Britain', *Economic Journal*, Vol. 61, 1951, pp. 544-61.

[3] Edward Nevin, *The Mechanism of Cheap Money*, Cardiff: University of Wales Press, 1955; Susan Howson, 'Cheap money and debt management in Britain, 1932-51', in P. L. Cottrell and D. E. Moggridge (eds.), *Money and Power*, Basingstoke: Macmillan, 1988, pp. 227-89.

extent that long-term government securities and private sector advances were considered substitutes by bankers (offering alternative means of employing bank sector funds), the government's funding policy pushed up the supply of the former and may, therefore, have crowded out private sector finance to some extent.

However, the banks' own pricing policy also played an important part.[1] At this time the clearing banks (with the tacit agreement of the authorities) operated a cartel, exercising effective oligopoly power to fix interest rates on both deposits and advances. The minimum rate normally operating on advances was set at 5 per cent per annum for 'prime accounts'. During the 1930s, however, market rates fell to historically low rates, leaving the inflexible cartel rate at an uncompetitive level. Indeed, Nevin has suggested that a significant number of bond holders, including business companies, sold bonds in order to reap the windfall profits from the rise in the value of their securities that had resulted from the general fall in interest rates.[2] Access to this source of cash, in itself, may have reduced the demand for bank finance. But more generally, the uncompetitiveness of the banks' cartelised price would have encouraged borrowers to seek alternative sources of funds. Indeed, the clearers lost market share to non-bank financial intermediaries.

Overall, then, continuity and conservatism are more evident in the deposit banks' general position than any radical shift in policy to cope with what many were declaring to be the unprecedented problems facing British industry at that time. The clearers remained firmly wedded to the need to maintain a highly liquid portfolio and (at least publicly) retained an aversion to long-term lending. They also remained loyal to an anti-competitive strategy that led to their exercising effective price control on their products and to confining their activities largely to the traditional areas they had developed in the pre-1914 period. In the result, they lost market share and, during the 1930s, made a smaller contribution to meeting the financial requirements of the private sector than in the previous period.

Nevertheless, as for the earlier period, it must be said that a great deal of the business of the banks remains undocumented. It is feasible, therefore, that despite the impression given by this overview of the banks' general position, the qualitative nature

1 Collins, *Money and Banking in the UK, op. cit.*, Chs. 7 and 8.

2 Nevin, *op. cit.*, pp. 250-51.

of bank lending changed in such a way as to offer substantial support to industry. Even if the figures suggest a reduction in the amount of support, it is still possible that the nature of bank lending to industry changed in a significant manner during the period. It is with this issue that the next sub-section deals.

The Nature of Financial Provision for Industry

There can be no doubt that the commercial banks were drawn more deeply into the problems of industrial finance on individual accounts during this period. This involvement arose mainly in response to the growing problems of industrial customers (especially in the export trades), with the banks having to take a more active rôle as the growing amount of industrial bad debt raised the danger of non-repayment of loans and, thus, threatened the value of the banks' own assets. As we have seen, there was also a more public dimension: the Bank of England, in particular, cajoled the commercial banks into initiatives where they could be seen to be doing something to help ailing industry.

A recent history of the largest of the clearers at the time, the Midland Bank, suggests that it was, indeed, very supportive of its industrial customers between the wars.[1] The authors also argue that considerations of commercial confidentiality made it impossible for the Midland to make public the extent of its commitment to industry, and that this contributed to the false impression of minimum involvement.

The Midland Bank and the Royal Mail Group

A major example of the Midland's commitment to industry is the case of the Royal Mail group of companies.[2] This entailed one of the bank's most important industrial 'rescue attempts', requiring deep involvement in the re-organisation of the group between 1931 and 1936. This important industrial group accounted for about 15 per cent of the country's merchant fleet (including the Royal Mail Steam Packet Co., Elder Dempster & Co., Pacific Steam Navigation, and the White Star line), and encompassed shipbuilding yards (including Harland & Wolff in Belfast) and steel production plants (such as Colville & Son in

1 A. R. Holmes and Edwin Green, *Midland. 150 years of Banking History*, London: Batsford, 1986, Ch. 7.

2 Edwin Green and Michael Moss, *A Business of National Importance. The Royal Mail Shipping Group, 1892-1937*, London: Methuen, 1982.

Scotland). The group was in debt to a number of banks, but the Midland and its affiliate, the Belfast Bank, were the main banking creditors with outstanding loans of almost £3·5 million. This commitment and the need to salvage as much as possible was to involve the Midland in five years of complicated, detailed involvement in the group's affairs, with senior bank executives devoting a great deal of time to the business strategy and plans of its large industrial client. According to Holmes and Green, this was but a spectacular example of many instances where the Midland showed the sort of deeper commitment to industrial customers for which the banks' critics were calling.

In fact, there is no shortage of examples of clearing banks providing substantial finance for—and/or being drawn into the re-organisation plans of—individual industrial customers. Most instances involved the declining industrial sectors, but there were also individual instances of important bank finance being provided to firms in new sectors such as motor vehicles. Examples of the latter type of help include Lloyd's assistance to the Rover Motor Company and the Midland's help to the Austin Motor Company.[1]

In addition to action on behalf of individual customers, the commercial banks were also involved in a number of well-publicised collective attempts to improve financial facilities for industry. As we have seen, most of these were carried through under the auspices of the Bank of England, with the commercial banks participating to a considerable degree, for example, in the financial provision for the Lancashire Cotton Corporation and the Bankers' Industrial Development Company.

A Critique of the Banks' Role

Recently Duncan Ross has attempted a systematic assessment of lending practice and involvement with industry by two of the country's biggest banks, the Midland and Lloyds.[2] He, too, is impressed by the extent of commitment portrayed by these banks. Nevertheless, he accepts that they did not provide

---

[1] See, for instance, Roy A. Church, *Herbert Austin: The British Motor Car Industry to 1941*, London: Europa, 1979; and James Foreman-Peck, 'Exit, voice and loyalty as responses to decline: the Rover Company in the inter-war years', *Business History*, Vol. 23, No. 2, 1981, pp. 190-207.

[2] Duncan M. Ross, 'The clearing banks and industry—new perspectives on the inter-war years', in J. J. van Helten and Y. Cassis (eds.), *Capitalism in a Mature Economy. Financial Institutions, Capital Exports and British Industry, 1870-1939*, Aldershot: Edward Elgar, 1990, pp. 52-70.

venture capital and that they formally tried to confine their industrial lending to short-term overdrafts. Nevertheless, he argues that some clients' problems were so severe, and the scale of the banks' prior commitments so great, that the banks were obliged to adopt a more active, participatory rôle—financing mergers where appropriate and taking on some managerial functions for the long-term re-organisation of some clients' businesses. He admits they were not initiators of industrial rationalisation but, in the trying circumstances of the inter-war period, they became involved to an unusual degree. His is a cautious, balanced judgement on the question of the nature of provision of industrial finance: 'the banks .... may well have been more permissive than active, but they were certainly not passive'.[1]

Some commentators offer a much less sanguine interpretation, however, and are much more critical of the banks' efforts. They argue that most, if not all, of the above illustrations of bank activity can be portrayed as 'minimum involvement', with the banks doing only what was necessary to protect their own assets, with little regard to the long-term interests of clients, let alone of the country. The banks are accused of maintaining their arm's length approach to industrial customers, of shying away from accepting greater managerial responsibility for the direction of customers' businesses, and of exhibiting little long-term commitment to the need for industrial restructuring.

A number of studies have been conducted, not from the perspective of the banks (as was the case for Holmes and Green, and Ross), but from that of the needs of industry; they tend to be more critical of the banks.[2] For instance, whereas Tolliday's study of the steel industry[3] admits that the banks were increasingly embroiled in the management of problematic customers, he is critical both of the degree of involvement and of the quality of the intervention. While admitting that the banks became involved to a greater extent than they were accustomed,

[1] Ross, *ibid.*, p. 66.

[2] John R. Hume and Michael S. Moss, *Beardmore. The History of a Scottish Industrial Giant*, London: Heinemann, 1979; Peter L. Payne, *Colvilles and the Scottish Steel Industry*, Oxford: Oxford University Press, 1979; Maurice W. Kirby, 'The Lancashire cotton industry in the inter-war years. A study in organisational change', *Business History*, Vol. 16, 1974, pp. 145-59; James Bamberg, 'The rationalisation of the British cotton industry in the inter-war years', *Textile History*, Vol. 5, 1988.

[3] Steven Tolliday, *Business, Banking and Politics. The Case of British Steel, 1918-1936*, Cambridge, Mass.: Harvard University Press, 1987, especially Part II.

this was, nonetheless, minimal. The banks engaged in detailed discussions with industrial customers only reluctantly, for instance when threat of bank losses made it necessary and, then, only to the minimum extent essential to protect the banks' assets. He claims that the banks had neither the expertise nor the inclination to embark on long-term programmes designed to restructure industrial clients' businesses. Indeed, the evidence from the steel industry is that, once their own assets had been secured, the banks withdrew what little managerial decision-making they had been contributing to industrial re-organisation.

Tolliday thus emphasises that, wherever possible, the banks stuck to their traditional rôle of providing short-term credit and that it was only the severity of industrial problems and the need to safeguard their previously committed loans that pulled them into any deeper involvement. Most other studies of the declining sectors reach similar conclusions, stressing that the banks' contribution to industrial re-organisation was reluctantly made, kept to a minimum and withdrawn as soon as industrial recovery made it feasible.

Conclusion

Thus, though the evidence is somewhat ambiguous, it does seem to suggest that it is reasonable to portray the bank/industry relationship of the inter-war years as not markedly different from that of the pre-1914 period. The main difference was that, in a number of important instances, economic difficulties drove the banks and industry closer together, involving the banks more deeply in their clients' own business affairs. The 'political' dimension was also relevant enough for the banks—and especially the Bank of England as guardian of the system—to be conscious of the danger of outside interference and to portray their own actions in the best possible light.

If one accepts the critics' view that British industry required a thorough restructuring at the time, and that the indebtedness of industry to the banks put the latter in a strong position to carry through such a restructuring, then the banks' actions were inadequate. In that sense, the banks of the inter-war period can be said to have failed industry.

However, such a conclusion follows directly from a certain set of prior expectations of what is considered 'reasonable' conduct for a deposit bank. If a more limiting yardstick is applied, a different conclusion follows. Two major points should be emphasised in the case of the inter-war years:

1. It is not obvious why deposit banks should be expected to take on the responsibility for industrial rationalisation, even if such a need was (and is) widely perceived. Why should such banks have broken with tradition, developed new expertise and undertaken (what was for them) the extraordinary risk associated with the task of managing and financing a restructuring of the industrial base? Deposit bankers had both the security of their depositors and the interests of their shareholders to protect. If an 'industrial transformation' was required in the period, is it not more reasonable to argue that the function lay with the industrialists themselves?

2. Criticism of the British banking system must be tempered by the knowledge that the policies adopted by the banks and the Bank of England avoided any liquidity crises of the sort that seriously disrupted such economies as the USA and Germany in the 1930s. Even if the cost of conservatism on the part of British banks was to deny industry better long-term financial facilities, an important bonus to the whole economy, including industry, was to avoid the trauma of serious bank failures.

VII. POST-1945 PERIOD

Criticism of the City and the clearing banks stretches back as far as the late 19th century, and is still prevalent today. Even in apparently enlightened academic circles there is a deep-seated belief that the City has somehow directed the allocation of funds in the economy to the detriment of industry. Yet there is possibly less reason for holding that view about the recent past than for any other period in the history of the City.

This section begins by adverting to a number of features that make the post-1945 world different from earlier periods. These features were both macro-economic and micro-economic, and they have provided an environment much more favourable on both the demand and the supply sides to the raising and provision of bank finance. There then follows a brief discussion of institutional arrangements which permitted easier access to medium- and long-term finance.

Internal Finance

As already explained (above, pp. 30-32), in the 19th century the bulk of firms' investment funds came from retained profits. It is not possible to be precise about the extent of this self-financing, but there can be some confidence that the overwhelming bulk of funds came from such retention. It has also been shown, however, that significant amounts came from external sources. Much the same is true in the post-Second World War period. Chart 1 shows that over the post-war period, although the series bumps around a great deal, retained profits as a proportion of total capital employed were invariably in excess of 60 per cent and on occasions more than 70 per cent. Bank borrowing as a percentage of total capital funds fluctuated around a mean of about 18 per cent (Chart 2), leaving the balance to be found elsewhere. The relationship of retained profits to total funds has therefore been remarkably steady.

Next, it will be shown that the contribution of the banks increased as compared with earlier periods. There was more medium-term lending and closer ties were established with customers. More convincingly, for the recent past there is some

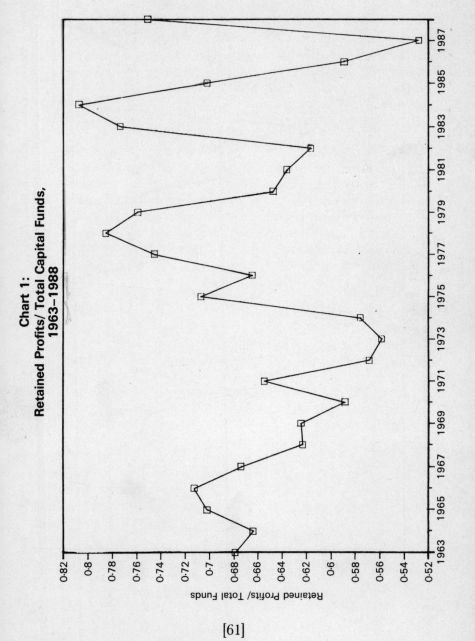

Chart 1:
Retained Profits/ Total Capital Funds,
1963–1988

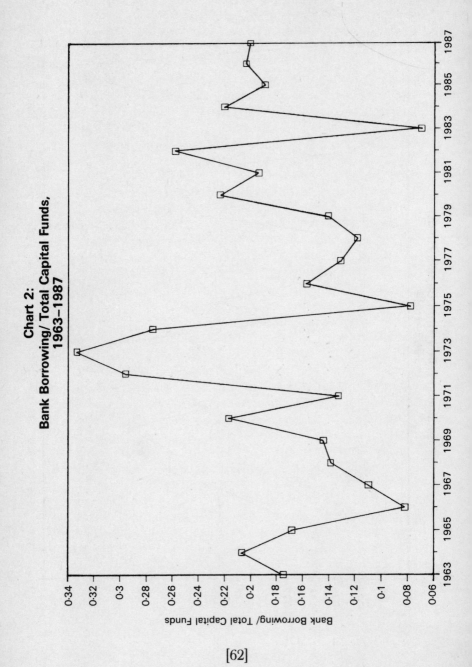

Chart 2:
Bank Borrowing/ Total Capital Funds,
1963–1987

Bank Borrowing/ Total Capital Funds

more rigorous analysis which supports the view that British banks do not compare unfavourably with European banks. When this is coupled with the very good stability record of the British banking system, it seems to us that the evidence points to some redemption of the much reviled London banker.

Changes after 1945

The world after 1945 has been considerably different from the period 1870-1945, and a number of the differences have had beneficial consequences for the provision of industrial finance. Macro-economic differences include the scale of personal savings, and the rate of inflation. Micro-economic differences include the new institutional arrangements for the provision of finance, and the structure of industry itself.

Apart from war and immediate post-war years, there had been no inflation of any consequence in Britain prior to 1945. Inflation, however, has persisted throughout the world since 1945, and it is now clear that inflationary pressures had been present since the 1940s. Inflationary expectations were greatly increased after 1970 when the entire world resorted to fiat money. The temptations for government that accompany such a régime effectively make inflation inevitable.

Rising inflationary expectations took hold at an early point after 1950. Periods of inflation affect investors and borrowers differently. The simplest view is that debt is more popular during inflationary periods. This view of course depends upon the assumptions that inflation is not being fully anticipated and is not cancelled out by rising interest rates lagging changes in inflation.

In addition, it is possible that inflation affects choices between bond debt and equity finance. Here the argument is more complicated but has important consequences for the question of bank provision for industry. In an inflationary period, if a firm's costs and revenues rise in line with inflation, dividends can be maintained in real terms. The value of a share would therefore be a hedge against inflation. The opposite applies to bonds: as interest rates rise bond prices fall and, therefore, one might expect a shift in the composition of assets from bonds to equity during unanticipated inflation. However, there are several reasons why a move to equities and away from debt may not occur, such as differences between relative and general prices, the effects of taxation, and so on. In 1981 the introduction of index-linked gilts was an attempt to make bonds a hedge against

[63]

inflation; it was not altogether successful since supply did not match demand. But over the post-war years as a whole the pressures are likely to have been such as to make equity finance more attractive, and hence to ease the pressure on the banks to provide debt finance.

Bank Liquidity High in Aftermath of War

Another factor that proved favourable immediately after 1945 was that bank liquidity was very high. Huge bank deposits and liquid asset holdings had been built up during the War and continued in the 'cheap money' period of the mid-1940s. It was a time, in other words, when—within the confines of government controls—the banks were 'asset driven'—that is, they were looking for loans to make to match their liabilities. Liquidity remained high for more than a decade and while it is difficult to make a precise estimate of the contribution this made to the banks' ability to supply finance to industry (Matthews, Feinstein and Odling-Smee suggest it was small),[1] at least it must have been positive. Against that, government controls on bank lending were probably relatively greater in the 1950s. When the physical controls and rationing of the War and immediate post-war years were eventually dispensed with, however, greater reliance was placed on controls such as those on bank lending.

A separate factor that probably operated favourably over most of the post-war period was capital controls: although they were not comprehensive and not wholly effective, controls on capital exports lasted until 1979 and probably kept the cost of capital lower than it would otherwise have been. Judgement on this issue must, however, be reserved in the absence of the necessary research. Individuals may have altered their savings habits, and foreigners may have viewed our capital market differently.

An indication of the supply of savings in relation to investment in an economy can be derived from the external accounts. The current account of the balance of payments is by definition equal to the excess of savings over investment. The British accounts show that from 1870 to 1930 there was a large current account surplus almost every year with the exception of wartime. It was in the years before 1914 that Britain accumulated a huge stock of foreign assets. The 1930s saw the first deficits of the modern period but after 1945 the current account

[1] Matthews, Feinstein and Odling-Smee, *British Economic Growth, op. cit.*

was back in surplus and remained so, apart from a few years, until the 1980s. So, on the evidence of the current account balance, there seems to have been no change of real significance in total savings behaviour in relation to investment in the economy that might affect this investigation. All these macro-economic factors relieved the banking system of some of the demand for funds.

On the micro-economic side, Rybczynski has argued that the changing structure of industry reduced the demand for funds, while increased financial innovation improved the supply of funds.[1]

Many factors after 1945 helped to provide a more favourable environment for industry to borrow funds, but the favourable aspects should not be overplayed. Many borrowers went to American banks operating in Britain or to hire-purchase companies, paying higher interest rate charges, which suggests that loans for more risky ventures were difficult to come by.

Institutions

In addition to the macro-economic and micro-economic environment described, several new institutions evolved which were designed to ease the financing problems of the small and medium-sized firms. To the extent that they were successful, it can be seen that there would have been even less for the clearing banks to do.

There had been a great deal of pressure for action in the 1930s following the identification of the 'Macmillan gap'—the gap in capital market provision said to exist for medium-sized companies seeking external finance.[2] In the mid-1930s three potentially important institutions were set up—Charterhouse Industrial Development Co. Ltd., Credit for Industry, and Leadenhall Securities Incorporation. Several other smaller institutions also appeared, but it was not until after the Second World War that a serious attempt was made to establish an institution which would devote itself specifically to small industrial and commercial issues. This was called the Industrial and Commercial Finance Corporation (ICFC), whose shareholders comprised the English and Scottish banks and the Bank of England. The banks

1 T. M. Rybczynski, 'Structural changes in the financing of British industry and their implications', *National Westminster Bank Review*, May 1982, pp. 25-36.

2 [Macmillan] Committee on Finance and Industry, *Report*, Cmd. 3897, London: HMSO, 1931.

contributed according to their size (measured by deposit liabilities), but left the day-to-day management to the Corporation. The principal aim of the ICFC was to

> 'provide credit by means of loans or the subscriptions of loan or share capital ... for industrial or commercial business ... where existing facilities provided by banking institutions and the Stock Exchanges are not readily or easily available.'[1]

By 1958 it had five branches, and by the mid-1970s that number had risen to 18. ICFC catered for large firms. A sibling institution, the Finance Corporation for Industry (FCI), concentrated on making loans to small firms.

Given that the corporation was set up to cater for smaller loans—generally thought of as being in the region of £100,000-£200,000—it may be thought of as moderately successful since by the mid-1970s it was lending at a rate of £25 million per annum, although on average that is only 150 loans of about £167,000 per loan.

The ICFC, set up in 1945 to fill the Macmillan 'gap', became part of Finance for Industry in 1973, an institution whose resources were greatly enlarged in 1974 when £1,000 million was made available by leading financial institutions, to enable the Corporation to provide more medium-term lending (covering a period of some seven to 15 years). In the mid-1970s another institution, Equity Capital for Industry, was set up with a similar objective at the initiative of the British Insurance Association and designed to appeal to the small issuer. Interestingly, both the FCI and Equity Capital developed the ability (and used it), to monitor the progress made by companies who borrowed from them. The most rapidly developing area in the 1970s and 1980s has been the unlisted securities market. Bank of England estimates suggest that by 1990, venture capital was being provided to around 700 companies which employed some 1·5 million people, and the scale of lending was running at over £1 billion per year.

The Banks

Advances Ratio

When considering the banks' contribution to industrial finance, a good starting point is their 'advances ratio'—that is, the proportion of their assets allotted to loans and overdrafts. Before

1 W. A. Thomas, *The Finance of British Industry, 1918-1976*, London: Methuen, 1978.

the First World War the banks claimed they aimed for a 50 per cent ratio, which seems to be very close to what they achieved: a ratio of around 48 per cent seems to have held from as early as 1880 up to 1913. Not surprisingly, the ratio fell during the First World War so that by 1918 it was down to 29 per cent. It bounced back almost immediately after the War and for most of the inter-war years was over 40 per cent, although it was on a downward trend in the 1930s. There followed another, not surprising, steep decline in the ratio in the Second World War— this time down to 15 per cent. Following that War, however, the ratio did not bounce back quickly: not until the 1960s did it rise above 40 per cent. By the mid-1960s it was back to what might be regarded as its normal or desired level in the high 40 per cent region; then from the late sixties until the late eighties it settled at around 50 per cent (apart from a brief, sharp rise to around 70 per cent in the early 1970s which is explicable in terms of 'round tripping' as a result of legislation). Thus, in broad ratio terms the banks behaved in a consistent fashion across a period of more than a century, aiming for (though not always successfully) an advances ratio of close to 50 per cent.

The debate is in good part about to whom the advances went, on what terms, and, importantly, for how long. Unfortunately, for much of the post-Second World War period there is no precise information on how the proportions of these loans and advances made to manufacturing industry differed from previous times. There is reason to believe, given some scattered evidence, that they stayed roughly in line with the pattern of the inter-war years when the banks made half of all their loans to industry, and that many or most were short term but were often rolled over to become in effect medium or long term. Still awaiting research is the question of who the recipients were and, more importantly, who the disappointed applicants were. What is certain is that in the 1960s the clearing banks became more active in medium-term liabilities and, to keep the balance sheet symmetrical, they increased their medium-term lending.

Regulations

To return to the explanation for the pattern in the advances ratio, the basic reason for the behaviour of the ratio after 1945 was the subjugation of bank behaviour to the perceived greater needs of government finance. The banks held large amounts of liquid assets after the War (see above, p. 64). The Government wanted to keep interest rates down and was launching its nationalisation programme. Government concern for servicing and funding the enlarged national debt coloured all its policies towards financial markets, including the banks. In particular, the clearing banks were effectively obliged to hold an historically large proportion of their assets in government securities. In the immediate post-war period, too, the Capital Issues Committee (CIC) laid down the guide-lines for the use of advances. Three times in the first few years (1945, 1947 and 1949) the CIC issued directives, and this restrictive climate persisted for most of the next decade. Further, by the mid-1950s the first quantitative restrictions on bank lending were imposed, to be followed soon after by a (relatively small) call for 'special deposits'. In 1964 the Bank of England laid down loan priorities which essentially meant that the finance of exports had priority and anything that smacked of speculation should be avoided.

In addition, the bank cartel of the inter-war years continued after 1945 and the cosiness was, indeed, fostered by the Bank of England which liked to use moral suasion in the exercise of monetary policy. In return for complying with the Bank's wishes the clearers were, for example, given exemption from publishing their profits. In 1958 the return to sterling convertibility had the eventual effect of opening up the London financial markets a little; at the same time other financial institutions were expanding. In 1971 the abolition of the cartel following the introduction of the policy of 'Competition and Credit Control' released the clearers from the restraints of cash and liquidity ratios which had clearly become too onerous, restrictive and dated.[1] New, less restrictive reserve ratios were introduced, and even though short-term economic pressures were to oblige the Bank of England to re-impose temporary restrictions on bank lending in the form of the 'corset' (1973), this was less distorting than earlier rationing.

Thus the 1950s and 1960s were decades in which the activities of the banks were closely restricted by the authorities. In the 1970s changes were made so that by the 1980s more market-oriented behaviour was permitted.

The banks had formed a loose cartel by the late 19th century and this had not been discouraged by the monetary authorities. In fact, the cartel was much tighter by the 1920s. The Bank of

[1] 'Competition and Credit Control', *Bank of England Quarterly Bulletin*, June, September, December 1971.

England's use of moral suasion in exercising monetary policy meant it found it more convenient to deal with a few bank chairmen situated physically nearby. The 1930s saw the cartel strengthened still further and this persisted into the post-Second World War years.

There were of course costs as a result of the deviation from competitive conditions, some borne by the monetary authorities (in this case mainly the Treasury) and some by the banks themselves. The principal cost was the tax effectively imposed by the requirement to maintain a cash/deposit ratio of 8 per cent (and a liquid assets ratio of some 28-30 per cent). On the basis of subsequent developments in the 1970s and 1980s, such reserve ratios now appear to have been far in excess of what the banks would have chosen for themselves if operating in a free, commercial environment. The total cost can be estimated by taking the amount of reserves held between the banks' preferred ratio and that imposed, and multiplying the difference by the return on Treasury bills. Such costs have been shown to be quite substantial, but the main cost is the loss of social welfare in the form of the higher price paid for the product that results from lack of competition. There may not have been a very large loss here (depending on the contestability of the market), but estimates suggest that the banks were certainly less efficient than they might have been.[1]

On the positive side, as in earlier periods, the British system delivered considerable financial stability. Cash and near-cash assets were large enough to meet any likely contingency and the whole system was underpinned by the Bank of England's close concern and its traditional rôle of lender of last resort. Such gains for the community must offset at least some of the losses from the operation of the clearing banks' oligopoly.

Inquiries

Such was the concern over industrial finance in the years after 1945 that it was the subject of regular investigation and inquiry. All the serious investigations in the period (Radcliffe, 1959; Prices and Incomes Board, 1967; Bolton, 1971; and Wilson, 1980)[2] reached conclusions which were moderately favourable

---

[1] Prices & Incomes Board, *Bank Charges*, Report No. 34, Cmnd. 3292, London: HMSO, 1967.

[2] [Radcliffe] *Committee on the Working of the Monetary System*, Cmnd. 827, London: HMSO, 1959; PIB, Cmnd. 3292, *op. cit.*; [Bolton] *Small Firms: Report of the Committee of Inquiry on Small Firms*, Cmnd. 4811, London: HMSO, 1971; [Wilson] *Committee to Review the Functioning of Financial Institutions*, Cmnd. 7937, Vols. I & II, London: HMSO, 1980.

towards the banks. In general, they found that there was no reason to regard the cost of capital or the availability of external finance as a greater obstacle to investment in Britain than elsewhere.

Radcliffe was generally sympathetic to the clearing banks and also praised the Industrial and Commercial Finance Corporation. At the same time, it pointed to a gap between the seven-year time limit imposed on loans by the clearing banks and the 15-year minimum of the finance houses.[1,2] The Prices and Incomes Board inquiry on bank charges was critical of the absence of price competition amongst the big banks. However, like Radcliffe, the Bolton Committee (1971) also absolved the clearing banks of blame for failing to provide funds. The Radcliffe Committee had recommended the reduced use of overdrafts and the extended use of fixed-period loans, and by the time the Wilson Committee reported in 1980, this had indeed been done. Radcliffe accepted that the facilities for financing investment had grown substantially since Macmillan reported (partly as a result of private institutions such as Charterhouse), and they did not advocate any further proliferation of institutions, either public or private. 'On the contrary, we believe that ... the existing institutions can look after the ordinary requirements of small businesses for capital' (para. 940). Its concern was with the availability of information on the institutions. Radcliffe also accepted the bankers' own evidence of their supportive stance:

> 'The joint stock banks are very important in the finance of small business, not only as a major source of capital but because the ordinary business of banking establishes a close contact between businessmen and bank managers which puts the bank manager in a unique position to help and advise the businessman on his financial affairs.' (para. 941)

But more importantly from our point of view, the balance of the evidence was that

> 'though the bank advance is conventionally a short-term loan, the banks do in fact lend on a large scale to such customers to finance medium-term and long-term requirements' (para. 941).

The Wilson Committee suggested that an area of difficulty

---

[1] Collins, *Money and Banking in the UK, op. cit.*, p. 446.

[2] As we have noted (above, p. 66), this particular issue was addressed later when the ICFC's resources were increased in the 1970s to allow it to fill this gap.

that seems a sensible conclusion. The assertion that the London Clearing Banks have been guilty of 'short-termism'—that is, being excessively wary of long-term loans and guided rather by short-term considerations—may be difficult to disprove but it is equally difficult to prove. There is no doubt, however, that the credibility of the assertion has been badly damaged recently.

It is perhaps ultimately impossible to disentangle the demand and supply effects and to measure the less tangible factors such as attitudes and the interaction difficulties between industrialists and bankers. But the evidence for the post-Second World War period is that, apart from there being a favourable environment for industry to obtain funds largely as a result of exogenous macro-economic factors, there were also several direct attempts to correct the identified deficiencies of the pre-war world. The most obvious of these was the creation of the ICFC. Consequently, there was less for the banks to do, whereas in practice they did more (especially more medium-term lending). All the serious investigations in the period show that there was a continuous improvement in financing provision, and the most recent and rigorous analysis of the question lends support to the view that the differences between Britain and other countries are not great now, whatever they might have been in the more distant past.

VIII. CONCLUSION

In 1870 Britain was the largest and richest economy in the world. Thereafter it went into relative economic decline, which was inevitable as new entrants appeared, more countries developed, and comparative advantages shifted. Explanations for the relative weakening of Britain's performance abound, but the rôle of the banks in financing activity has usually been prominent amongst them. Whether or not the banks' behaviour resulted in lower investment, and whether that led to poorer economic growth rates, are long-debated issues. It is difficult to believe that profitable opportunities would not attract the appropriate institutions into the market, especially over a long period. But it is nevertheless important to remember that institutional constraints do operate and can show considerable inertia.

British banks have been attacked from many sides and for various types of failure but central has been the criticism that they were always overly concerned with liquidity. The evidence is, however, ambiguous. There were shocks to the system, such as that of 1878, which had at least the temporary consequence of scaring banks off long-term industrial lending. But the changing structure of the system and experience in the economy can hardly have allowed a change in attitude to have persisted perversely, or even to have been widespread.

The long-term perspective in this *Hobart Paper* shows that the nature of the relationship between the banks and industry has varied over time. Before the First World War there was little formal commitment of long-term finance by the banks to their industrial clientele. Nevertheless, extensive short-term credit facilities were provided and renewals of short-term loans and overdrafts were used to carry customers over long periods. Moreover, it seems that lack of greater involvement by the banks was due more to reluctance on the part of most industrial firms to seek additional outside funds.

The problems and opportunities of the inter-war period were to provoke a greater degree of bank/industry co-operation, but it is doubtful if this constituted a fundamental change in the nature of the relationship. Also at that time, the operation of the bankers' cartel added to the uncompetitiveness of the money markets. Since then, however, there have been serious attempts at forming institutions to remedy the deficiencies, and recent comparisons between Britain and Germany—the two supposedly contrasting examples—show little difference in magnitude of provision by the banks of finance for industry.

British banks learned lessons in the mid-19th century that other countries' banks came to accept later. A series of mid-century financial crises resulted in bank failures when banks were too heavily committed in long-term loans to firms. There was undoubtedly some change in lending practice. There is no evidence that industry suffered a shortage of finance.

Moreover, while the banking system became increasingly concentrated from the 1870s onwards and became an effective cartel from the early 20th century, and that resulted in costs, there was an important benefit. The benefit was *financial stability*, upon which economic progress depends. The structure was one of a small number of heavily branched banks with well-diversified portfolios. No financial crisis occurred in Britain after 1866. Most other European countries, the USA and others suffered repeatedly severe damage to the real economy as a result of financial crises.

QUESTIONS FOR DISCUSSION

1. Are British banks over-cautious?

2. Chart the path of conservatism in British banking over the past century.

3. Which banking 'model' is more conducive to economic growth—the European or the British?

4. The argument that banks have failed rests on the belief that lack of industrial finance damages investment and hence economic growth. Do you agree?

5. Did inter-war economic problems bring about a lasting change in bank/industry relations?

6. What were the principal costs and benefits of the British banking cartel?

7. How have the needs of government finance impinged on the composition of commercial bank sector assets during the 20th century?

8. Assess the success of the various British institutions specifically designed to provide industrial finance.

9. Would you agree that the British case shows that some reticence on the part of banks to become involved in the commercial affairs of clients is a prerequisite for financial stability?

10. Have British banks been overly concerned with overseas interests?

FURTHER READING

Best, Michael H., and Jane Humphries (1986): 'The City and Industrial Decline', in Bernard Elbaum and William Lazanick (eds.), *The Decline of the British Economy*, Oxford: Oxford University Press, pp. 223-39.

Confederation of British Industry (1987): *Investing for Britain's Future: Report of the City/Industry Task Force*, London: CBI.

Collins, Michael (1988): *Money and Banking in the UK: A History*, London: Croom Helm.

Cottrell, P. L. (1980): *Industrial Finance, 1830-1914*, London: Methuen.

Griffiths, Brian (1973): 'The Development of Restrictive Practices in the UK Monetary System', *Manchester School*, Vol. 41, pp. 3-18.

Kennedy, William P. (1987): *Industrial Structure, Capital Markets and the Origins of British Economic Decline*, Cambridge: Cambridge University Press.

Mayer, Colin (1987): 'Financial Systems and Corporate Investment', *Oxford Review of Economic Policy*, Vol. 3, No. 4.

Ross, Duncan M. (1990): 'The Clearing Banks and Industry: New Perspectives on the Inter-War Years', in J. van Helten and Y. Cassis (eds.), *Capitalism in a Mature Economy: Financial Institutions, Capital Exports and British Industry, 1870-1939*, Aldershot: Edward Elgar, pp. 52-70.

Sayers, R. S. (1976): *The Bank of England, 1891-1944*, Cambridge: Cambridge University Press.

Thomas, W. A. (1978): *The Finance of British Industry, 1918-1976*, London: Methuen.

Training Too Much?
A Sceptical Look at the Economics of Skill Provision in the UK
J. R. SHACKLETON

There is still a consensus that British workers are unskilled in relation to their foreign counterparts and a considerable increase in government expenditure on training is required if our relative economic performance is to be improved. This consensus exists even though it is difficult to find any positive correlation between the resources a country devotes to training and its rate of economic growth.

State expenditure on training has risen from less than £1 billion in 1978 to nearly £3 billion in 1991 without any thought being given to the economic principles which should govern such expenditure. As a result, a large government-funded training industry has emerged, depending significantly on increased contributions from the taxpayer. The author also argues that the new Training and Enterprise Councils (TECs) have become pressure groups calling for more state spending on training. If there has been a market failure in training, is it legitimate to argue that more money ought to be spent centrally? It is possible that the government is already spending too much on training or is diverting expenditure into the wrong channels. Unless there is clear evidence of the extent of market failure, we cannot judge whether the government is doing too much or too little to assist training provision.

Education and training are vital to the economic prosperity of a nation but whenever government action is suggested as a remedy for market failure, the extent to which government fails should also be considered. Governments do have a powerful incentive to be seen helping the labour market at times of high unemployment but we should be sceptical of those who claim to know the labour market's training needs better than the individuals and firms involved.

ISBN 0-255 36307-9 Hobart Paper 118

The Institute of Economic Affairs
2 Lord North Street, Westminster
London SW1P 3LB
Telephone: 071-799 3745

£6.95